Ethnic Jewelry

Other Arts and Crafts Books by Dona Z. Meilach

SCULPTURE

Contemporary Art with Wood
Contemporary Stone Sculpture
Creating Art with Bread Dough
Creating Modern Furniture
Creating Small Wood Objects as Functional Sculpture
Creating with Plaster
Creative Carving
Decorative and Sculptural Ironwork
Direct Metal Sculpture *with Donald Seiden*
Sculpture Casting *with Dennis Kowal*
Soft Sculpture and Other Soft Art Forms

FIBERS AND FABRICS

Basketry Today with Materials from Nature *with Dee Menagh*
Contemporary Batik and Tie-Dye
Contemporary Leather
Creating Art from Fibers and Fabrics
Creative Stitchery *with Lee Erlin Snow*
Exotic Needlework with Ethnic Patterns *with Dee Menagh*
Macramé Accessories
Macramé: Creative Design in Knotting
Macramé Gnomes and Puppets
Making Contemporary Rugs and Wall Hangings
A Modern Approach to Basketry with Fibers and Grasses
Plant Hangers
Soft Sculpture and Other Soft Art Forms
Weaving Off-Loom *with Lee Erlin Snow*

COLLAGE-PAPER

Accent on Crafts
Box Art: Assemblage and Construction
Collage and Assemblage *with Elvie Ten Hoor*
Collage and Found Art *with Elvie Ten Hoor*
Creating Art from Anything
Papercraft
Papier-Mâché Artistry
Printmaking

CERAMIC-TILE

Tile Decorating with Gemma

DESIGN

The Artist's Eye
How to Create Your Own Designs *with Jay and Bill Hinz*

ALSO

The Art of Belly Dancing *with Dahlena*
Jazzercise *with Judi Sheppard Missett*
Homemade Liqueurs *with Mel Meilach*
How to Relieve Your Aching Back

DONA Z. MEILACH

Ethnic Jewelry
Design & Inspiration for Collectors & Craftsmen

WITH PHOTOGRAPHS BY DONA AND MEL MEILACH

CROWN PUBLISHERS, INC.   NEW YORK

Inquiries should be addressed to Crown Publishers, Inc., One Park Avenue, New York, New York 10016

Printed in the United States of America

Published simultaneously in Canada by General Publishing Company Limited

Library of Congress Cataloging in Publication Data

Meilach, Dona Z.
    Ethnic jewelry: Design & inspiration for
collectors & craftsmen.

    Bibliography: p.
    Includes index.
    1. Ethnic jewelry. 2. Ethnic jewelry—Influence.
3. Ethnic jewelry—Collectors and collecting.
I. Meilach. II. Title.
NK4890.E86M44   1981   739.27   80-21240
ISBN: 0-517-529742

Book design by Dona Z. Meilach

10 9 8 7 6 5 4 3 2 1

First Edition

Contents

Acknowledgments

Gathering material for this book has been a long and delightful task. Though a labor of love, it has also required inordinate energy: energy spent traveling and photographing the objects in various countries as well as that spent in research and writing. Traveling to all the countries where ethnic jewelry is made and worn would be impossible, so I have had to draw on the resources of several other people, their expertise, their photos and their private jewelry collections.

I am particularly indebted to Barbara (Mrs. Wayne) Chapman of Solana Beach, California, whose vast collection and knowledge of jewelry were a marvelous sharing experience. I am grateful to Sol Gurevitz of the Field Museum of Natural History, Chicago, who made the museum's collection of photos available to me. What was not available, he arranged for and permitted me to photograph without any limitations.

I wish to thank the many other museums, private galleries and collectors who shared with me photos of pieces in their collections or allowed me to photograph pertinent examples. Credit is given where applicable. In several instances, private collectors preferred to remain anonymous.

Thanks to my son, Allen Meilach, for the lively drawings illustrating how jewelry is worn by different cultures.

I bow to and acknowledge my husband's contribution, his assistance with photography, and his time spent in the darkroom developing many of the photographs snapped in "available light" conditions. Mostly I want to thank him for his help and patience while traveling. Some of the situations where we photographed pieces could become skits for stand-up comedians. We were lucky to leave Morocco with our cameras still in our possession. He deserves extra bouquets for learning to suppress winces every time I saw a piece of jewelry I had to have.

I want to thank my typists, Collette Russell and Penny McBride, for their help in deciphering my drafts. With so many words new to them, they performed beautifully.

And to my editor, Brandt Aymar, my continuing gratitude for his enduring enthusiasm for ideas I present in the briefest outlines. I

admire his stoic patience as he waits for the manuscripts and over-
sees and guides production with unerring attention to detail and
design. This is our twenty-third book together, which may set
some type of record.

DONA Z. MEILACH
Carlsbad, California

NOTE: All photographs, unless otherwise credited, are by Dona and
Mel Meilach.

Ethnic Jewelry

1
Introducing Ethnic Jewelry

Combining the jewelry of many cultures into one book is like tasting a wide selection of aperitifs at an international buffet. You can select, contemplate, digest and enjoy the individual pieces that appeal to your eye and taste. You can go back for more when you determine your favorites.

The ingredients for this intercontinental jewelry buffet depend on tribal jewelry, on ritual items, Oriental pieces and others, with elements that have been created by a society and a tradition handed down from one generation to another. The pieces may seem vastly different, varied and exotic to the Western viewer. In reality, within one society there is not so much variety; the use of pieces is not so free and creative as we might imagine. The number of chains worn by a young woman may be rigidly prescribed by custom, the beaded necklaces added to only on certain occasions; specific stones and types of jewelry may be worn only by high-ranking people and dignitaries, to symbolize their authority.

In many cultures, jewelry communicates messages: love, hate, power, hierarchy, aggression, pride, birth, growing up, virginity, maleness, femaleness and more. How and why jewelry is worn on the body every day and in special rituals and ceremonies are among the fascinating aspects of this study.

Written information about the magic and the symbolism of individual beads and stones, strings of silver, shells, carved bones and other objects is sparse and sometimes contradictory. But beads and jewelry are considered in the realm of a folk art so that the usage is verbal and handed down from generation to generation with the stories changing, the symbolism altering by situation and time.

I have offered some of this symbolism where I have been able to document it through personal interviews during my own visits to the countries or with researchers who have had intimate contact with the people or the pieces. Yet often when I was told an authentic analysis of the intent of a single bead or piece of jewelry, it was questioned by someone else whose knowledge was based on close contact and/or study of a group. Ethnologists who have lived with some of the tribespeople offer what they have seen of an object in use. They shrug their shoulders when another theory is offered.

Opposite:
A pair of grand silver fibulae with chased and engraved details. Round and square cabochons are set into bezels. Coins and silver beads dangle. The pin portions are hinged. Photographed in Marrakesh, Morocco.

A stone arrowhead-shaped pendant and oval bead with an engraved leaf design. Africa.

There is no way to check it through. What may be ritualistic or symbolic in one group could have a minutely different meaning for another living within a short distance or farther away. The passage of time and outside influences can alter meanings, too, just as they do in our own societies and religions.

I have tried to avoid showing examples of a culture where the designs became faddish and so popular that they were being reproduced in quantity for the marketplace by merchandisers in another country. In recent years, for example, American Indian jewelry became instantly collectible. Beautiful tribal squash-blossom necklaces, jade and wampum, carved shell and bone birds and other pieces were rapidly reproduced in imitation materials in countries with cheap labor and the ability to copy. The imitations were marketed at roadside stands in the West, and they spread across the continent. So much was written, in depth, about American Indian jewelry during that period that I elected to show only museum examples of early tribal Indian jewelry. The reader is encouraged to look for specific books on American Indian jewelry if that area is of particular interest.

The study of ethnic jewelry can be approached from many avenues. The anthropologist and ethnologist will seek the meaning behind the pieces; they hope to learn about the behavior of the group and the individuals within the group.

The jeweler may study the pieces for techniques, combinations of materials, methods and motifs. He will observe the designs on a bead or the shape and design of a total piece and how tiny portions or an entire piece can inspire something for his own work. There is often a naïveté in primitive jewelry design that is refreshing and appealing to our culture. In the early 1900s, Pablo Picasso and Georges Braque interpreted the simplicity they saw in African masks into sculpture, and a new art movement was born. So too may this observant approach to a collection of ethnic jewelry be interpreted by designers.

The contemporary artist-craftsman may seek and search for the motifs and patterns used by a particular tribe that carry over into the allied crafts of the group: wood carving, stone carving, ceramics, weaving, body painting, needlework, baskets and others. Sometimes it is difficult to isolate the study of only one medium because pattern is persistent and interconnected.

Fashion designers may discover new ideas as to how jewelry may be worn. The "total body adornment" appearance of many tribal groups as opposed to a simple single strand of pearls is delightful. Usually there is a reason. The Bedouin tribes of the Moroccan desert, for example, are nomadic and have no jewelry boxes in which to store their wealth, so it is worn on their bodies at all times.

In most tribal cultures jewelry is also a sign of a woman's status and the ability of her husband to provide for her, so it must be worn where it can be seen. The size, weight and numbers of chains and amber beads worn would make us wonder at the ability of a woman to walk around with the pieces. They seem to manage beautifully, often juggling a heavy burden on their heads at the same time.

Opposite:
Many Egyptian jewels seen in museums are beautiful in design and craftsmanship. We can study how they were worn only by observing the sculpture, paintings and other artwork that have endured from a given time period. The necklace, headwear, belt adornments, bracelets and their design motifs show in the carved slate "Palette of King Narmer," from Hieraconpolis, 3200 B.C. The leaf design carved in the animal ears transcends time and country. It is similar to the recent carving on the African pendant on page 1.
Courtesy, Egyptian Museum, Cairo

A woman of India wears large earrings with two portions. One small set of rings may hang from the pierced earlobe; a large ring may be clipped over the top cartilage of the outer ear. Often the ear is pierced at the top and center as well as in the lobe. Several necklaces may be worn simultaneously. Together they aid in a visual balance for the full-skirted garment.

Among the Masai of Africa and some of the primitive groups of India, colorful and large neckware is used to offset the visual body balance of women where custom dictates that heads be shaved.

Body adornment is not always confined to people. Some Ethiopian jewelry is made to be worn by animals. The pieces jangle in the same tradition as our cowbells; the owners know where goats and camels are when they hear the tinkle of the bells. The same styles are worn by the people.

Regarding jewelry, men in a tribal society are much more flamboyant than are men in our society. Much has to do with the male's hunting prowess, virility and status within the society.

Observing the effect of jewelry worn in many cultures can shatter some of the "fashion rules" about how to wear jewelry foisted upon our society under the guise of up-to-date fashion. There are articles that dictate, for example, that "a woman only five feet tall must wear small jewelry close to her chin; anything longer would make her short and dumpy." That is a narrow, erroneous viewpoint. A short woman with long jewelry can appear tall and elegant if she is careful about the background display she uses for that jewelry. I have seen a short, stylish woman look stunning laden with almost as many pieces as the Berber girl on horseback. She has taken care to wear a simple, unadorned garment and to pull her hair back to show off and emphasize her jewelry. She is like a walking art form, a moving canvas that expresses her taste in her choice of jewelry. She wears her jewelry as in a beautiful portrait that will never age.

Collectors of ethnic artwork will also discover details in the pieces illustrated that may enable them to identify a bead, a pendant, a material. Such details will help them seek out and to select the pieces they want for a specific assortment. This familiarity may introduce them to individual beads or types of materials they might not have seen before. As more and more people tune in to the value of the pieces, their worth is likely to increase.

Caution is emphasized if you plan to collect ethnic jewelry for investment. Unscrupulous entrepreneurs have already discovered how easy it is to re-create "antiques" that people will buy quickly. It is not unusual to visit a back village in Bali or Thailand and observe a group of artisans making instant antiques that are exported to America and Europe as "authentic antiques." It is difficult to tell the difference unless you know from handling one piece in relation to another that the weight of the silver, the shine on the beads and the way they are put together differ between old and new. New pieces are often thin and poorly welded; the string may be a shoelace rather than the sinew used by the original societies. The quality of the craftsmanship is often inferior as the elements are reproduced in a primitive version of production pieces.

Don't overlook the fact that there are still skilled craftsmen making quality pieces today, often as a family in a generation-to-generation tradition. Such craftspeople and their work can be discovered with time, patience and research.

I have learned the differences in objects after handling much of the jewelry myself. The pieces I bought years ago in a specific country simply because I liked them, not knowing about them for

The ceremonial jeweled headwear of Empress Theodora is shown in this detail of her costume portrayed in mosaics on the wall of the Church of San Vitale, Ravenna, Italy, about A.D. 547. The ornateness of the piece helps establish the empress's rank compared to the simpler jewels worn by her attendants. In several pieces the shape of a fish appears; it is among the most frequently repeated symbols in jewelry from many cultures and religions.

In studying the designs of a country, it is often fascinating to observe the repeat overall impessions and motifs that occur in the stone, wood and metal sculpture and in the paintings.

Top:
A recent carved wooden puppet head from a Balinese traveling troupe repeats the shapes and interior designs in the bead-work and sequins on the headdresses of the fabric dance costumes (see page 90).
Collection, Mr. and Mrs. Wayne Chapman, Solana Beach, CA

Below:
A limestone Bodisattva of the Tang Dynasty, A.D. 618–906, China, is adorned with a simple necklace, armbands and bracelets.
Courtesy, The Art Institute of Chicago

Jewelry of the Mayan cultures differs markedly from the Far Eastern cultures in design and how it is worn. Motifs on the belt of the figure in a carved limestone wall panel from the late Classic period are still used today. The elements and the symbolism combine to inspire the contemporary craftsman as seen in the necklace, *(opposite).*

Courtesy, Field Museum of Natural History, Chicago

any reason other than their appeal to me as beautiful and different pieces of jewelry, now appear to be of a finer quality than most imported pieces I find today.

Another aspect of native jewelry is not only the varying interpretations given as to the symbolism but also stories that collectors relate. I had seen several examples of antique Thai jewelry in a museum; identifying captions suggested that the pieces were very rare and dated back a hundred or a hundred fifty years. A subsequent visit to Thailand and the northern hill tribes where the jewelry was made taught me an important lesson. The same quality pieces of jewelry were still being made, still labeled "antique," and allegedly dating back one or two centuries. When I suggested this to one of the salespeople, he simply shrugged and suggested that they give the people what they want to hear. The styles are ancient, so what more is important?

When compiling material for this book, I observed that examples in some museum and private collections were identical to the pieces I had photographed during my travels. Some of the pieces had been fabricated recently because they continue to be used by a society and the styles do not change. This is not always so. An object that is no longer in use could be an authentic antique. A flint pouch, for example, may no longer have any use by a society so it is no longer made. But, then "antique" is not the sole reason for collecting.

It is exciting, fascinating, to study jewelry by itself. It is even more revealing to study the myriad ways it is used. Where possible, I have shown the jewelry being worn in either photos or drawings; I have also illustrated other art forms of the people, such as painting and sculpture. Often it is only through other art forms that we learn about habits of former societies. The same is true of jewelry. We can study the stone palette of the ancient Egyptian kings and learn much about the people's dress habits in addition to the historic aspects we may have focused on in college art-history courses.

I remember studying ancient Egyptian stone pieces to determine the position of the legs and body and how the artist portrayed the human figure. During my college days, it did not occur to me to study the pendant, the belt buckle, the hair ornament. Assuming that other people may have missed observing these details during their own studies, I have included examples of artwork from many cultures that can illustrate how jewelry was worn.

Certainly this is not a new approach in relation to Byzantine, Greek, Roman and other European art. Through the centuries, costume jewelry and precious jewelry have been inspired by the paintings and sculpture of a given period. During the United States tour in the late 1970s of the exhibition of the jewels from the tombs of King Tutankhamen, a rash of Egyptian-styled jewelry flooded the market from the dime-store variety to almost priceless ornaments heavily gemstone-encrusted.

The history of jewelry reveals changes in styles based on the interest in various cultures throughout the ages. One can find brief surveys and detailed historical views of jewelry among the books listed in the bibliography. A historical survey of jewelry is not the premise of this book.

Ethnic jewelry is offered for reasons already mentioned, but I want to underscore the following: Each time the jewelry is studied, it may be looked at for different reasons. A first glance through the examples may impress you with the tremendous variety of style. The second reading will reveal the variety of motifs and symbols, and within the variety there is great repetition. The fish, for example, is a recurrent theme; yet it is used with as much variety as fish made by nature herself. The reason for the repeat of the fish motif is not so complicated. Non-Christian and pre-Christian societies deem it a symbol of fertility and good luck; Christian societies see it as a symbol of Christ (see pages 34 and 35.). The Japanese carp

A silver necklace from Taxco, Mexico, 1965, repeats the motifs found throughout the centuries in Mayan stone sculptures, paintings, photographs and manuscripts.
Collection, Dona Meilach

Masked dance figures of Mexico are often depicted wearing earrings, pendants, belt decorations, feathers and other objects that symbolize ideas portrayed in the dance.

suggests virility, and a fabric replica is flown from rooftops and flagpoles as a symbol of boys' day.

You may wish to study the geometry of the jewelry in one analysis and observe how many pieces are based on the circle, the square, the triangle, the crescent and minor variations and combinations. Another thumbing through will reveal the tremendous variety in the types of findings used to hold a dangling pendant or bead to another element; the Chinese use silver or twine in the shape of an eternal knot, which is symbolic of their culture. In other pieces a single loop, an S-curve, or a rosette over a joining makes it decorative.

Finally, a study of the types of chains and links can be of vital interest to a jeweler. I know one contemporary jeweler who prides himself on having made a study of the types of links used in every culture he could discover from early Greek to the present. He has duplicated each of them. Short examples of single-loop chains to multiple-braided chains in any number of configurations hang from a four-foot-long dowel rod in his studio. He is still discovering more varieties in the jewelry, the arms and armor of Renaissance warriors.

Designs of the glass beads made by the Venetians, East Indians, Dutch, Romans, Nigerians and other societies and used for trade beads in Africa have been the subject of entire volumes of books, scholarly papers and magazines devoted to beads. The story of the bead can thread its way through almost every culture in every period of time. Beads have permeated societies from ancient and primitive man to the present for their beauty, as a magical charm to ward off evil or to bring happiness and for countless other reasons.

The single bead is a fascinating basic element of a society. It is created, combined with other beads, traded and brought to other countries in a cross-culturization. Amber from Africa appears in Japan; ivory from Japan emerges in Afghanistan. Ancient Chinese pieces carried across the world by travelers are lusted after by Europeans. The beads of South America are copied by the Mexicans; the ceramic beads of Mexico are found in California, where they were brought by explorers.

This opens another chapter in the story of beads. One reason they have so permeated various societies far removed from their origin is because of their relatively light weight and portability. The magnificent Venetian glass beads were used as money in trade with Africans. When tiny, colorful seed beads were introduced into America, the Indians quickly traded skins, fur and land with European traders for the beads. Beads were the medium of barter.

Techniques used in the creation of ethnic beads offer another insight to the character of jewelry from around the world. The domed silver bead is a basic unit of construction with many variations. By placing a shaped strip of metal between the domes, an openwork bead results; and the variation in openwork styling is apparent in many examples. It is interesting to note that one can often determine the country where a bead originated by the type of openwork; craftsmen tend to continue in the tradition of the country. The pierced bead from Mexico has one style, the bead from Guatemala another. An openwork bead from India is distinctly different from one from Japan. The differences are obvious—not

Loops and coils are popular in the jewelry of many cultures. They are worn as necklaces, earrings, armbands, bracelets and ankle rings.

Opposite, top:
A young girl from the Meo hill tribe, Thailand, wears a four-coil silver collar.

Opposite, bottom:
Young women of the Padaung tribe, eastern Burma, wear neck coils that weigh about 20 pounds and measure about a foot high. In daily living, the brass loops are further adorned with strings of pearls, gems and silver chains with dangling coins. A small pillow under the chin is used for cushioning. The women may also wear brass coils on the legs from ankle to calf as well as shorter bracelets. One explorer referred to the women as "giraffe women." A physician, Dr. John M. Keshishian, studying the effects of the elongation of the neck, concluded that the practice pushed down the chest, clavicles or collar bones and the ribs; the vertebrae were not actually elongated. The jewelry, as in many cultures, is a sign of elegance, wealth and position.
Collection, Field Museum of Natural History, Chicago

Bronze cast figures of the Benin Tribe, Nigeria, sixteenth century, exhibit the use of coils around the neck.
Courtesy, Field Museum of Natural History, Chicago

Women of the Masai tribe, southern Kenya, encase their wrists in wire coils similar to the brass coils worn by the Burmese women of the Padaung tribe. Masai women wear colorful beaded collars and huge earrings to offset their shaved heads (see page 133).
Courtesy, Jay and Lee Newman from Wire Art, Crown Publishers, Inc.

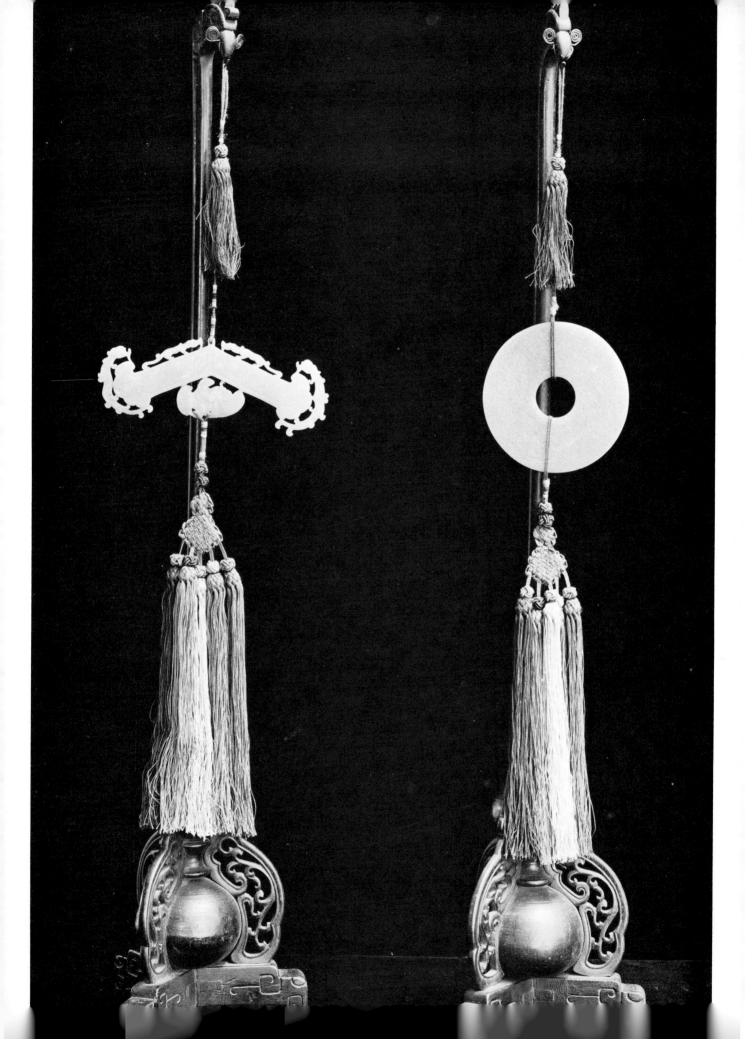

Ancient jade circles and other geometric shapes are found among artifacts of ancient China, probably from the middle Chou period (782–421 B.C.). There is controversy over the precise meaning and use of the shapes. The pi (circle) was the symbol of heaven; the others were symbols of earth.

The Chinese have not used gold and silver massively, nor is personal adornment as popular as it is in many other cultures. Carved jade is probably the best-known precious material used in early China, and during the Shang dynasty (1523–1028 B.C.) pieces of jade were incorporated into sculpture or worn as badges of office or rank. Many jade circles were found in tombs, and magical properties were attributed to them. The objects were believed to prevent the decomposition of corpses. Flat, round and square disks with a center hole were a common form that symbolized heaven and eternity. The disks were usually plain until the Chou period (1027–256 B.C.), when carved decoration appeared.

Opposite:
Left: White carved jade on a wood stand with silk tassels. China. *Right:* The white jade disc was a badge of rank. China.
Courtesy, Field Museum of Natural History, Chicago

Jade circle with designs is probably of the Sung period (A.D. 960–1279). The Sung period was a time of artistic flowering; paintings, pottery and other art forms were intricate and sophisticated, yet the symbolism of ancient times was persistently used. The carved design in the center bottom is a repeat of the interlaced animal mask motif, the "tao-t'ieh."
Collection, Field Museum of Natural History, Chicago

In Kyoto, Japan, a metalworker carefully taps shapes of gold and silver into grooved metal for pendants and other objects in a process called Damascene (see page 98).

even subtle—when you begin to observe them. Beads from Morocco may have colored enameling on them; those from the tribes of Afghanistan can be more ornate and elongated than those from Ethiopia. You get a feel for the subtle differences, and soon you will be able to identify them. This book will help you focus on these details and make you aware of what to look for.

You will also learn that the basic jewelry techniques are universal; only the design applications are different. These are defined on pages 16 and 17. An ability to recognize embossing, repoussé, pierced work, filigree, enameling, cloisonné and other techniques will enrich your knowledge and appreciation of what you are studying. Knowledge of the working techniques will help you identify pieces regardless of the country and give you a framework for cataloging them.

Finally, if you enjoy jewelry for the individual pieces themselves, you may take a cue from some of the contemporary craftsmen-collectors. They, like the ethnic peoples, want to show off the treasures they have.

You may not be able to find an authentically strung elegant necklace once worn by a young Moroccan girl from the southern Sahara Desert nor may you be comfortable with a pound or more of heavy amber around your neck. You may want to show off a few of the beads you treasure. You can combine your beads for a contemporary ethnic look that will result in an ageless individual

Moroccan men wear decorative objects as body adornment instead of traditional jewelry. The techniques used to create them are the same as those used for other silverwork. A flask design is chased with domed elements. It is worn slung over one shoulder and across the chest where it is accessible.

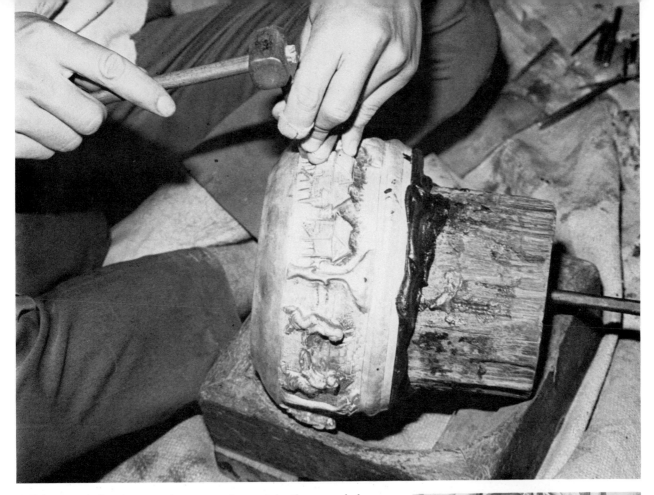

A Balinese metalworker seated on a wooden mat on the ground shapes sheet metal into a round form and creates the design in deep bas-relief by the repoussé process. The metal form is worked over a bed of pitch held by a log. Bowls, platters, jewelry, are decorated in the same fashion when repoussé techniques are used.

piece. Style is dictated only by your own good taste and preferences; and if you tire of a piece, you have only to cut it apart and re-string the beads in a new arrangement.

Begin to collect an ethnic necklace, an ethnic bead. Many are available individually from bead sources or from your own purchases when you travel. Perhaps you will find some of these pieces in your own jewelry drawer collecting dust. The necklace of beads you bought in a foreign bazaar might seem trinkety or touristy in its entirety. Cut it apart and combine beads from one area with those from another culture. Don't be afraid to use whatever you have in a new arrangement that appeals to your own aesthetics, your own color and size preferences. String them on dental floss, rattail, leather laces or shoelaces. Anything. If you string them with appreciative care and an attention to detail and line, you will achieve a vitality and energy similar to those that permeate the ethnic ethic of jewelry.

As you learn to appreciate the beads, the stonework, the silver from ethnic jewelry, you will learn to associate one with another until you are pleased with the arrangement for your own purposes.

Whichever single or multiple aspects of ethnic jewelry appeal to you and to your specific interests, I hope you will enjoy the examples offered here as much as I have enjoyed photographing, collecting and displaying them for your appreciation.

The men of Morocco wear the fine white ceremonial jellaba with a beautifully fashioned silver dagger and case hanging at the hip by a silk cord. The curved, bladed highly ornamental weapon is as much a part of their dress as a tie is in our culture.

13

TYPES OF BEADS

Beads are the basic element of jewelry. From the tiniest shell to large shapes of copal amber that defy one's neck to hold them up, they are still beads. Whether small or intricate, sliced shell or precious stone or silver, they have been used to purchase men and land; yet they are taken for granted, and little is known about many of them. Beads may be made from a rich assortment of materials native to a country or they may have been traded or brought to a culture through various routes. For the purpose of study, it helps to organize the beads into bead groups.

Assorted Natural Materials

Natural material: Seashells, seeds, pods, quills, bones, horn, teeth, stones and gems from the sea or the land.

Some may be used as they come from nature; others require that holes be drilled. Seeds may be carved or painted; shells and horns may be sliced. Stones and gems may be shaped and polished.

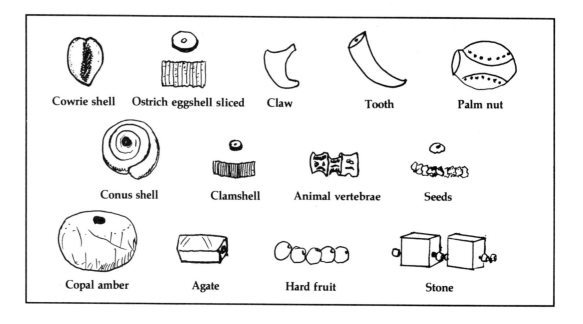

Glass Beads

Glass beads, often called "Venetian" beads because so many were made in Venice, come from other parts of Europe, and India,

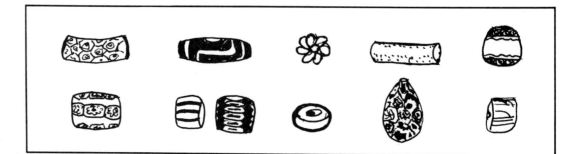

as well. Glass beads are made in a dizzying assortment of shapes, colors and combinations; collecting and studying such beads is a lifelong endeavor for the intrepid bead collector. The glass beads often used for trading have permeated societies throughout Africa and the Americas. Colored and patterned large beads were treasured by the Africans and appear in their showy "trade bead" necklaces. American Indians favored smaller seed beads, which they sewed onto their clothing and also strung into single strands of many colors to be worn as necklaces or belts.

Assorted Beads of Silver

Beads of silver are used extensively in the African and Middle Eastern cultures, and representative examples from Afghanistan, Ethiopia, Pakistan, Morocco and other nearby areas are shown.

The following silver bead designs appear throughout the book, and you will soon be able to recognize them with their many variations: Amulets with granulation, openwork beads, domed beads, rosettes, fish, arrows, hands, coins, and small silver boxes in triangular, rectangular and half-moon shapes sometimes delicately embroidered with silver filigree.

An Ethiopian necklace *(at right)* contains many of the elements found in silver jewelry from African and Eastern countries: the range of silver beads and chains, the prayer holder box used as a pendant, a round stone set in a silver bezel at the front, a smaller version of the box of stone at the back, domed and openwork or pierced pieces, square agates, carnelian and small silver beads.

Clay and Wood

Clay beads are made in a variety of stylized shapes such as birds, fish and other symbolic forms. Many are from Mexico. Wood beads may be round, oval, square or triangular and vary in size and types of wood.

Collection, Doña Meilach

Above:
Fine lines are made by "engraving," heavier linear designs by "chasing."

Center:
An example of "repoussé": The design is made from the back of the metal to result in a relief on the front surface. Additional "chasing" is accomplished from the front for detail.

Right:
"Dapping" is illustrated by the half-round dome in the center of the rosette. For the many silver beads shown throughout the book, two halves of a dome are soldered together. Round "coiled" wire is used to attach the drops to the rosette.

BASIC METALWORKING TECHNIQUES

The basic jewelry-making techniques are applied to the metalwork and other materials, where applicable, throughout the book. When you are familiar with the techniques you will be able to detect how they are used, varied and combined.

Recognizing the methods for fabricating and decorating jewelry will give you a greater appreciation for the work. Craftsmen in some cultures are known for specific methods; and, with experience, one can often rule out or pinpoint the country of origin by the techniques used.

CHASING — A metal surface is enriched with designs made by driving pointed tools into the metal with hammers. Chasing is often used in conjunction with repoussé.

ENGRAVING — Fine lines are cut into metal or other durable materials with sharp, pointed, chisel-like tools.

REPOUSSÉ — Metal is hammered, punched and shaped from its back with specially shaped tools. The result is a relief design on the front side.

DAPPING — Flat metal is placed in a concavity and hammered to conform to the shape. It is used for making domes and other rounded forms. A special dapping block is made of metal with different sized concave areas; the metal is shaped into the block with a round-tipped tool driven by a hammer. A dapping block can also be of wood or other solid material.

PIERCING — The negative "pierced" areas are removed from within a piece of metal by cutting or stamping out to yield the designs.

GRANULATION   Tiny beads or chips of metal or other material are fused onto a surface to create a relief tactile and visual design and texture.

LOST-WAX PROCESS   A casting method in which a wax or polyfoam model is made, then invested in sand or plaster. When molten metal is poured into the investment, the model burns out and the metal assumes the form of the model.

FILIGREE   A delicate design of fine wires that results in a lacy appearance. The wires are soldered together within the frame of a heavier wire which may or may not be placed on a metal base.

WIRE COILING   Flat or round wire is twisted to create a coil. Coils can be made in round and flat shapes.

FORGING   Metal is heated and hammered or twisted into a shape.

SOLDERING   The process of heating metals to their individual melting points, then adhering them to one another.

ENAMELING   Glassy substances are fused onto metals for a variety of effects: cloisonné, champlevé, plique-à-jour (see pages 100–101.

Left:
Several basic metalwork techniques are illustrated. The twisted wires are made by "forging"; the repeat curving wires create a lacy pattern by using the "filigree" concept; the small metal rounds illustrate "granulation." All the elements are "soldered" together and assembled.

Center:
An example of flat "coiled" wire.

Right:
The "lost-wax process" is used to cast the crosses. When a flat investment is made, it can be used many times for molten-metal pours.

2 Dimensional Metalwork

Ethnic jewelry made of metals reveals rich and abundant designs, shapes and detailing. Examples in this chapter emphasize forms made with dimension—domes, balls, tubes and so forth, compared with the flatter forms in the following chapter. Silver dominates because it is more readily available than gold or copper. Much of the tribal silver jewelry today is made from coins that have been melted down and reused. We actually saw silversmiths melting the coins in the jewelry-making centers of Thailand and Bali.

Symbolic shapes that appear in the jewelry, such as fish, birds, mandalas, rosettes, crescents, are usually echoed in other ornamentation. They are evident in the stone and clay work, in paintings, tile designs, weaving and embroidery too. Tradition is the norm, creative ideas are neither required nor desired among the traditional artisans.

In most societies the possession of jewelry is a sign of wealth and status. Certain types of pieces are reserved for wear on special occasions, but generally much of the jewelry is worn daily.

A visit to the Meo hill tribe in the hills of Northern Thailand substantiated this practice. Young girls and women wear their elegant silver neckpieces while performing their everyday chores, whether it is sewing or marketing. Even young girls, some less than six or seven years old, sat in the village roadway embroidering while the sun glistened on their tubular neckbands. The boys wore them while working in the fields and hiking on the highways. In the cities, one soon learns to identify the group to which a person belongs by the jewelry that is worn. Ornamentation makes people recognizable to members of their own group and unmistakably distinguishable from their neighbors.

The style of jewelry and its functions vary by country and custom. Sometimes individual pieces are functional as well as ornamental. There are prayer holders and message boxes, perfume and incense bottles, amulets and grooming tools.

Opposite:
Silver tubular coils with fish and other symbols are worn by the women, men and children of the Meo hill tribe, Thailand. Chains, bells, coins and other silver shapes are decorated with characteristic imagery. Earrings are pulled through the ear lobe, which may be pierced to accommodate two or more pairs of earrings.

A woman from the African Gold Coast wears huge gold pendants through her ears, a gold nose ring, neckpiece and forehead decoration. Amber beads are part of the headdress.

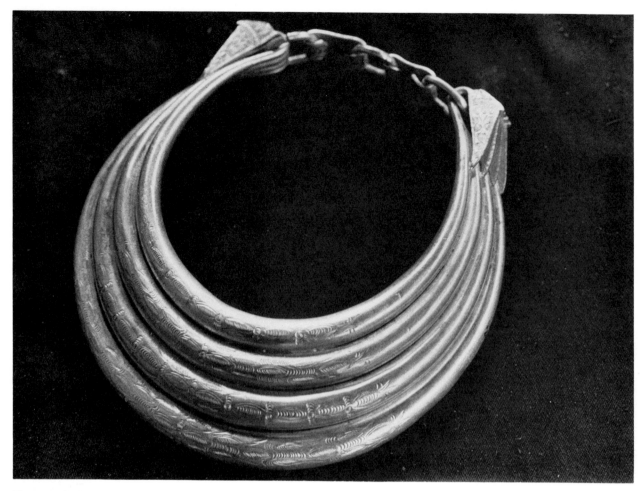

The typical silver neck coils worn by the Meo of Thailand may range from one to five or six rows graduated in size and held at the back by a large chain. The more valuable coils are intricately designed with stylized animal imagery.

The box form, which opens and closes in many of the pieces from India, remains a closed symbolic object in the Chinese culture. The box is a leitmotif threading its way . . . or holding its contents . . . in many societies. It can be made of gold or silver, plain or ornamented. It can be woven of leather, constructed or carved of wood or bone. It may be made as a container and not necessarily as jewelry, but it is ornamented as jewelry. Examples are the Japanese inro, Indian lacquer ware, the niello pillbox from Thailand and other countries where the technique is used. When a beautiful box is found, whether or not its original function is still important, it is a form sought by many collectors.

Throughout the book, examples have been selected to illustrate the variety and, where available, how the objects are worn by the people of the culture for whom they were made. You can focus on any aspect of the pieces that has special meaning for you, guided by your own interests and eye for design.

Women from the Akha, another northern Thailand hill tribe, used flatter jewelry elements for neckwear than those worn by the neighboring Meo. Their headwear is heavier and consists of silver balls and coins. The silver is worn with strings of colorful glass beads.

Above:

A young Thai woman from the Meo hill tribe wears a single neck coil and small earrings and accompanies them with a hair ornament made of beads and coins.

Left:

An ancient relief stone sculpture from India illustrates jewelry worn at the time: ankle bracelets, collar necklaces, heavy earrings, arm bracelets and a beaded girdle.

Below:

The clasps on bracelets and neckpieces from Thailand and other nearby countries are often in the shape of a symbolic pair of elephant heads.

Collection, Mr. & Mrs. Wayne Chapman, Solana Beach, CA

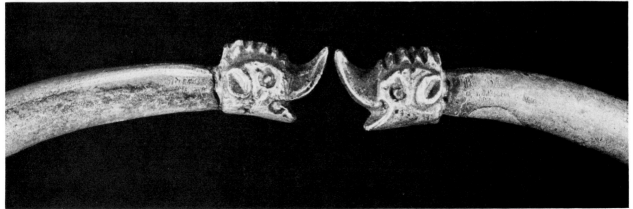

Domed silver shapes with stones, usually coral, set in the center are attached to a leather belt worn by women in Tibet.
Collection, Field Museum of Natural History, Chicago

A deep dome shape with repoussé designs has strings of pearls suspended from within. All are strung with silver beads. It is used as a pendant which may be worn as part of the headdress near the ears, as earrings, or attached to a necklace. Pakistan.
Private collection

A silver necklace from southern Afghanistan has a variety of elements including enamel crescent moons, stonework, Islamic coins and tassels.
Collection, Conway Peterson & Sons, Carmel Valley, CA

All color photographs are by Dona Meilach unless otherwise credited.

Assorted shapes and varieties of opaque amber beads are highly valued and worn by many tribal cultures. The amber beads are often combined with silver, bone, stone and other beads.
Collection, Mr. and Mrs. Wayne Chapman, Solana Beach, CA

A silver prayer or scroll holder with shell design beads is the pendant for a strand of silver and carnelian beads. Afghanistan.
Collection, Conway Peterson & Sons, Carmel Valley, CA

An armband, or bracelet, of silver with glass lozenges set in silver bezels. Kazakh, southern Russia.
Collection, Conway Peterson & Sons, Carmel Valley, CA

An Islamic prayer holder with intricate chased silverwork and silver and carnelian beads. Kazakh, southern Russia.
Collection, Peterson Conway & Sons, Carmel Valley, CA

A silver prayer holder in a box shape has calligraphy that is actually some of the prayers. It is strung with amber beads.
Collection, Peterson Conway & Sons, Carmel Valley, CA

A prayer holder box with a floral design that is repeated in the silver beads. Red carnelian beads. Afghanistan.
Collection, Conway Peterson & Sons, Carmel Valley, CA

An engagement necklace from Ethiopia. A variety of jewelry techniques are illustrated in this one piece of jewelry that exhibits the virtuosity of the craftsmen.
Collection, Dona Meilach

An antique necklace with a pendant made of a form of cloisonné. Straight silver wire and sliced pieces of shaped, hollow wire are soldered to a silver backing. The negative areas are filled in with enamel. Openwork and elongated chased beads are strung with opaque amber beads. Southern Russia, about 1800.
Collection, Dona Meilach

A lidded silver box with enamel work from Morocco. The purse-like box is used as a container and worn around the neck as a body adornment.
Collection, Dona Meilach

Turquoise, brass and pre-Columbian stones are strung as a necklace. Peru.
Collection, Dona Meilach

Tiny brass box-like beads with "shot" give the appearance of filigree. The beads, called "telsem," are strung on a blue cord and used for the birth ritual. Ethiopia.
Collection, Dona Meilach

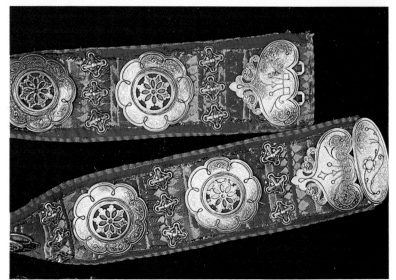

Openwork discs and beads are sewn to a handwoven belt. The designs are niello work. Bukhara, southern Russia.
Collection, Peterson Conway & Sons, Carmel Valley, CA

A beaded umbilical-cord holder in the shape of a turtle. American Indian.
Collection, Field Museum of Natural History, Chicago

A body adornment from Indonesia made from wood, brass, mirrors, beads and tassels. Such pieces are used in dance ceremonies and are quite large.

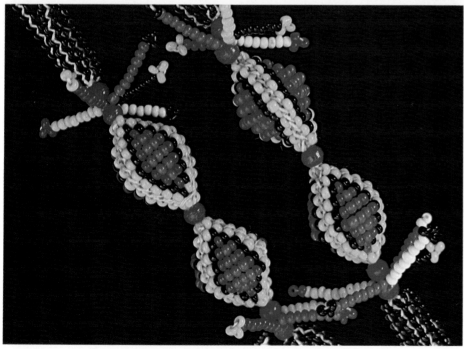

Three-dimensional woven beadwork (detail). Morocco.
Collection, Dona Meilach

"Pectoral with Ashanti Gold." Wrapped and woven silver and gold embroidery thread with linen, silk, wool and acrylic from different countries become the pectoral, or breastplate, adaptation in a contemporary neckpiece. It is combined with stones and beads from Africa, Israel, Brazil, Mexico, Italy and Tibet and an abalone shell from the Philippines. The title is derived from the gold color used in African Ashanti gold weights. By Helen Banes, Silver Spring, MD.

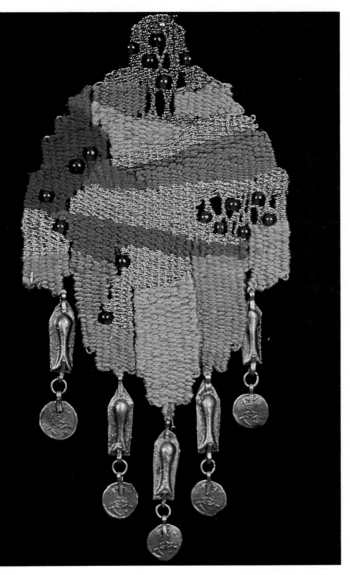

A modern adaptation of ethnic symbols. The Hand of Fatima is emulated in a fiber pendant made by pin weaving and combined with red beads. Silver fish and coins hang from the bottom edge. By Helen Banes, Silver Spring, MD.

Silver fibula pendant with a green glass button "jewel," red beads and Islamic coins. Morocco.
Collection, Dona Meilach

Silver pieces similar to those used on the belt *(opposite)* are worn by Tibetan women on woven fabric strips suspended from the head. The strips are a display area, and more pieces are added as they are acquired.
Collection, Field Museum of Natural History, Chicago

Right:
A cast tumbaga (gold-copper alloy) lizard pendant from Colombia, South America. Beads were probably added along the back after the casting was completed. In Colombia, the lizard represents knowledge, power and social correctness.
Collection, Field Museum of Natural History, Chicago

The gold nosepiece and earring worn by a woman of Nepal reflect a rosette design indigenous to Nepal and similar to those of adjacent countries. In India, among the wealthy, both men and women pierce their nostrils in order to insert large rings embellished with jewels or pearls. Some of these ornaments have little chains that attach to the hair. Other customs include inserting a rounded knob of gold or silver in one or more of the incisor teeth and wearing a jewel, usually a diamond, in the skin in the center of the forehead.

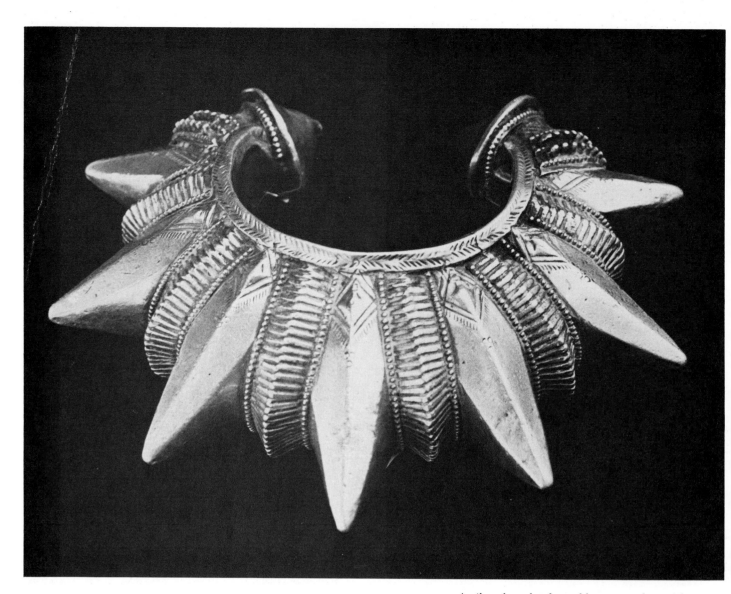

A silver bracelet for ankle or arm from Afghanistan is in the shape of the India crescent. The decorated bands are made separately and added between the protruding pieces. The assembly can be detected in the last band, right. The piece is 6″ wide, 2½″ high and 4½″ deep.

A silver dragon bracelet from northern Thailand exhibits Chinese influences. Many people in these countries are of Chinese descent, and their artwork often reflects their Oriental heritage.
Private collection

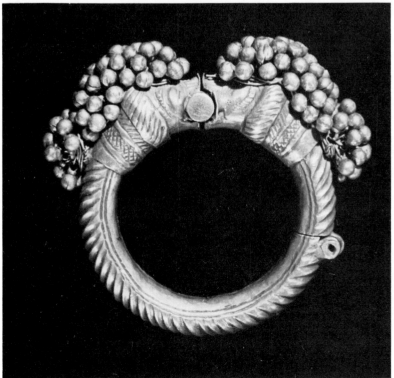

A pair of intricately designed ceremonial ear-rings from Morocco with stones and shot (tiny silver beads). The filigree-like design is created by soldering twisted silver wire onto the basic dimensional silver.
Photographed in Morocco

Bracelet, from India, is hinged, and the hinge at the center becomes a decorative element. Groups of silver balls are added with wire links.
Courtesy, Field Museum of Natural History, Chicago

A cast bronze ceremonial bracelet (two views) worn by an African chief. Such bracelets are extremely heavy and worn only on special tribal occasions. Their heaviness adds to the chief's status and are a symbol of authority.

Ankle or arm bracelet of cast bronze often worn by and used to identify a slave. It is very heavy.

Clockwise, starting at upper left:
Slave bracelet; the protrusions could have been used to attach a chain or rope. Ceremonial bracelet. Friendship bracelet, called a "ring" but worn on the wrist, is extended when shaking hands with another person to show that no weapons are carried. The ring is actually extended for the shake rather than is the hand, hence the term "friendship ring." Africa.

Upper arm bracelet, India. The carved design is entirely different from that of the African bracelet.

Poor man's bracelet. Made by the Africans to be sold to the poorer man; it is made of nickel rather than silver, copper or bronze.

One of a pair of silver armlets from Pakistan worn on the upper arm.
All examples: Collection, Mr. & Mrs. Wayne Chapman, Solana Beach, CA

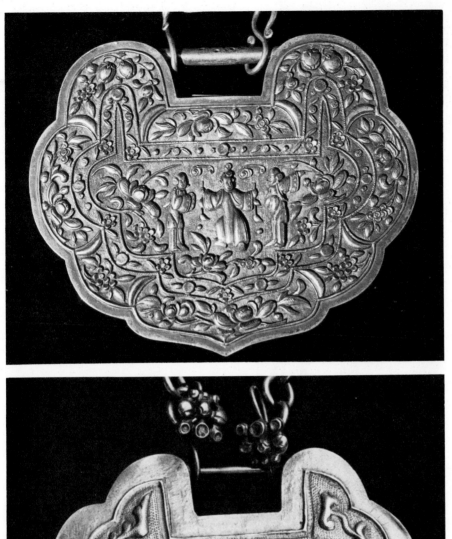

Opposite:
A large Chinese lock with a "bat" figure that represents conjugal bliss and which may have been presented at a woman's marriage.

The locks are usually made in a curving shape with a line repeated within as a border. The work is repoussé, with some chasing.
Collection, Peterson Conway & Sons, Carmel Valley, CA

Antique lock pendant, China, with the calligraphy developed in repoussé and chasing.
Collection, Mrs. Robert Rothschild, Northbrook, IL

In China locks are symbols of longevity and prosperity. The large intricately designed boxlike pendants are usually worn by the women; small ones are made for the children. Most have calligraphy or symbols that offer the wearer ten thousand years of happiness. The findings that hold the chain to the lock may be shaped as an eternal knot. Often such jewelry is presented to a woman on special occasions. The hanging beads are in symbolic shapes such as a bat or peach stone, that symbolize conjugal bliss. The mouse is a symbol of wealth based on the observation that the mouse goes only to the granary that is full; the full granary is owned by a wealthy person.

A brass box with applied enamel in black, red and gold on white ground. The box is hinged and probably made to hold a small prayer scroll. It hangs on a braided silk neck holder with a slide bead and a silk tassel. 1¾" long, 1¼" wide, ⅞" deep. India.
Collection, Dona Meilach

A Rajasthan, India, silver prayer holder opens from the back. One is often worn on the arm. A pair may be worn on each side of a headdress by women in southern Morocco in Tissant, south of Agadir, as shown in the drawing.
Collection, Mr. & Mrs. Wayne Chapman, Solana Beach, CA

Above:

Small purses made of different metals with wire filigree on solid backing are worn around the neck by the men and women of Morocco. Some areas are enameled. Designs vary but are always similar and repetitive.

Above, right:

The pendant is a silver prayer holder that contains a holy writing and is inscribed with verses of the Holy Koran. Believed to be from about 1780, Kazakh tribe, near Samarkand, Russia. It is strung with silver and amber beads.

Collection, Peterson Conway & Sons, Carmel Valley, CA

An octagon box *(right)* with a silver latch has a repoussé and chased design. It is worn by the Sadhu from Afghanistan and believed to be used to carry the prayer, written on rice parchment, from mosque to mosque. Approximately 2½" in diameter.

Collection, Peterson Conway & Sons, Carmel Valley, CA

A silver necklace from India is practical as well as decorative. The beads are amulet holders; the pendant is a scent bottle.
Collection, Field Museum of Natural History, Chicago

Pendants from Ethiopia with glass and carnelian beads are sometimes called "animal jewelry"; they originally hung around the necks of various livestock. The "bells" rang so the animal could be located.
Collection, Dona Meilach

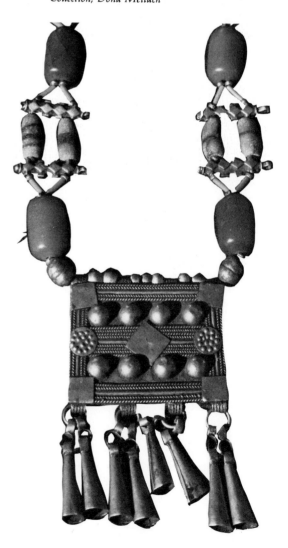

A necklace from Tibet with cast and hammered flat silver beads.
Collection, Field Museum of Natural History, Chicago

A Moroccan pendant represents the cross. One or more may be worn on a necklace with other pieces of silver coins, beads and amber. The circle, or dome, in different sizes and in positive and negative forms, is the repeat element.
Collection, Dona Meilach

Crosses as they are typically worn by the Berbers of Morocco. Prayer boxes, worn on each side of the head, are partially hidden by the large beads and coin jewelry.

A stylized fish repeats around a large necklace from Morocco. Each fish is made from two silver shapes made by dapping, or stamping. They are then silver-soldered together.

The fish is an often repeated jewelry symbol. In some regions the fish represents luck, fertility and a variety of good omens. In India, it is a sign of the firmament. In Christianity it is a symbol of Christ because the five Greek letters that form the word "fish" are the initial letters of the five words "Jesus Christ, God's Son Saviour." The fish is also a symbol of baptism, for just as the fish cannot live except in water, the Christian cannot live without the waters of baptism.

The three-dimensional fish form used in antique and high-quality pieces may have been completely handmade. In other pieces, the half-shapes are usually stamped out of silver in assembly-line fashion, and the two halves are assembled by soldering. The same practice is used for other shapes, too—the shell, lotus flower and so forth.

A fish made with the incised lines and inlaid niello work of the Bedouins of North Africa. Each of the attached coins has a different design.
Collection, Helen Banes, Silver Spring, MD

In Japan, the fish is a celebrated symbol for strength and for boys. A carp, associated with Boy's Day, is often made of intricately hinged parts so it moves. Silver with a twisted silver wire overlay.

Silver carp, Japan. 2½" long.
Collection, Dona Meilach

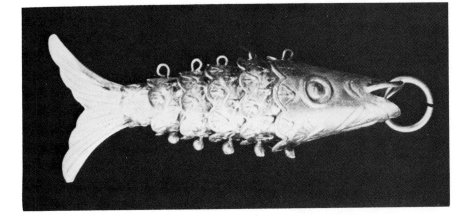

A necklace with fish- and shell-design pendants. The fish and shell are symbols of the earth in many cultures.
Collection, Mrs. Robert Rothschild, Northbrook, IL

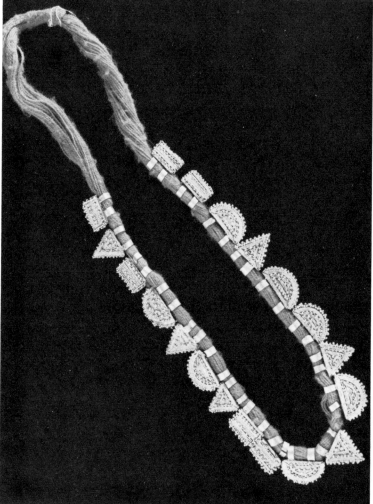

A necklace from Ethiopia with brass beads formed into boxes of different shapes. The twisted wire and tiny granulation result in a lacy-looking decorative and tactile element. Each bead measures only ¾″ to 1″ or ½″ to ¾″ and ⅛″ high. The beads, called "telsem," were presented to an infant, and new ones were added as the child grew. They are strung on blue cotton, which symbolizes the baptismal cord.
Collection, Dona Meilach

A gold-washed silver pendant prayer holder is strung with silver and cherry amber beads. From the Kazakh tribe of southern Russia.
Collection, Peterson Conway & Sons, Carmel Valley, CA

The young men of a primitive western India tribe, the Bondos, adorn themselves with an incredible amount and variety of metal, shell, glass and wood jewelry. Earrings are suspended from the top of the ear, and another coin earring is placed in the lobe.

A gold necklace from India with beads strung on braided cord with a tassel.
Courtesy, Field Museum of Natural History, Chicago

Above:
Metals, designs, size and how a bead is incorporated into a neckpiece help to identify its origin. This typical bead of the Berber of northern Morocco is well worn. Much of the enameling, which is usually combined with silverwork, has chipped away. If only it could tell a story, we would learn so much.

Left:
A simple openwork bead, mid-nineteenth century, Chinese.
Collection, Mrs. Robert Rothschild, Northbrook, IL

Opposite, top:
Silver pendant set with a gem crystal believed to be from the window of a holy mosque. The elongated beads are fertility symbols strung with cherry amber beads.
Collection, Peterson Conway & Sons, Carmel Valley, CA

Opposite, bottom:
An ankle bracelet from India exhibits a marvelous variety of bead forms: the prayer holder, round beads that emulate the forms on columns, amulet beads and coiled wire beads.
Courtesy, Field Museum of Natural History, Chicago

Far right:
A large silver bead on a necklace strung with amber, coins and smaller fluted and openwork silver beads. Detail. Afghanistan.
Collection, Dona Meilach

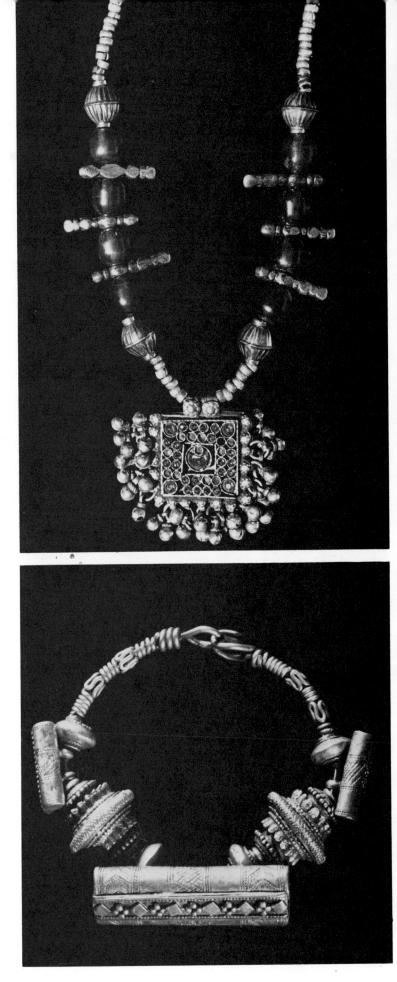

A prayer or scroll holder from Afghanistan with shell design drop beads on unusual chain links. It is strung with coral and silver beads. Such scroll holders open and close with a cap or an interior tube that slides out from one end. In India, similar but less ornate pieces were used to send messages with the servants from one house to a neighbor's house as the women were not allowed to visit one another. The ends of the holders could be sealed with lime to keep the messages from the servants. Essentially, such pieces were not made to be used as jewelry, but they have found their way onto necklaces.
Collection, Peterson Conway & Sons, Carmel Valley, CA

Opposite:
A formed and chased silver pendant with chains and silver coins from Morocco. Lacking a gemstone for the center, the creator incorporated a green glass button.
Collection, Dona Meilach

Opposite, far left:
A necklace, probably from Afghanistan or Nepal, made with round beads and rectangular boxlike beads with calligraphy. Silver. Round beads are strung both horizontally and vertically.
Collection, Mr. & Mrs. Wayne Chapman, Solana Beach, CA

Opposite, top and bottom:
Necklaces from India in the collection of the Field Museum of Natural History, Chicago, illustrate variations in the techniques and elements used. The top ornate silver and jeweled piece is combined with glass beads. Bottom necklace has jewels set within.
Collection, Field Museum of Natural History, Chicago

Right:
Simple, unadorned beads from Mexico of metal, wood and onyx strung in graduated sizes. Each bead is strung with coins between, with more coins used between the larger beads than between the smaller beads. Painted, colorful wood beads are interspersed with the onyx. Shapes and progressions may differ within one necklace.
Collection, Casa de Pancho, San Diego, CA

The bridal necklaces of the Turko-
mans of central Asia are unique.
They are brought down from Afghanistan and, according to sources,
are also called "generation" necklaces. The reason? The story is that
when a young girl is married she is
given a single strand of beads. She
hands this strand to her daughter on
her marriage, and another strand is
added. The necklace goes through
many generations and becomes the
dowry for a young girl. If hard times
force a woman to sell her necklace,
she believes her daughter will not be
able to marry.

The large beads are beautifully
and intricately designed with granulation and gemstones. Other beads
may be silver, coral, amber, glass.
Some of the pendants may be used
to hold prayers.

Many techniques are used for
forming the silver shapes, which
attest to the virtuosity of the silversmiths; sheet metal, chasing, forming, repoussé, granulation and
filigree can be seen.

The entire authentically strung
necklace with its many strands criss-
crossing is desired by collectors.
Many of the individual beads are
sought after by contemporary artists,
who delight in combining them in
the new necklaces shown in Chapter
7. Studying the authentic pieces can
suggest new arrangements for beads
and strands that are different from
the conventional single- and double-
strand necklaces. Details opposite
and right and on following pages.

Examples these pages: *Collection, Mr.
& Mrs. Wayne Chapman, Solana Beach,
CA*

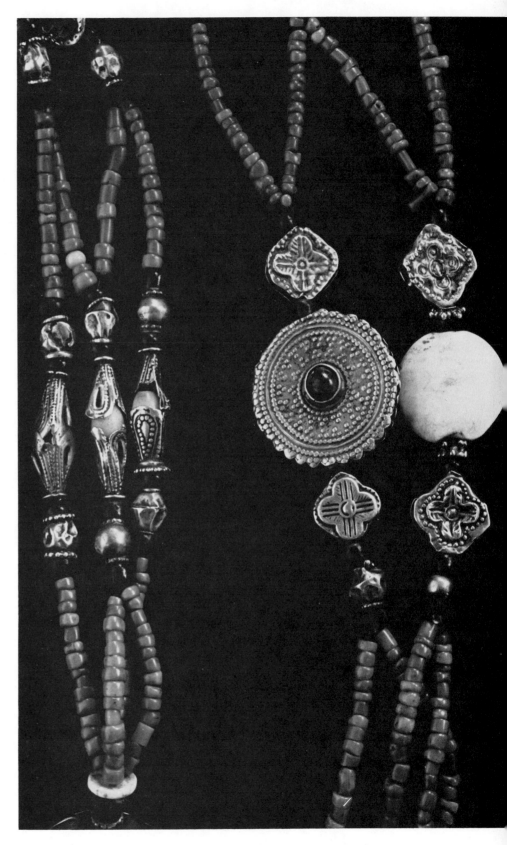

Turkoman bridal necklace with camel-
bone beads and a large silver bead, and a
bead and stone in a setting for the pendant.
*Collection, Mr. & Mrs. Wayne Chapman, So-
lana Beach, CA*

Bridal necklace. Afghanistan or Turkoman.
Observe the different arrangements of the
strands in all the examples.
*Collection, Mr. & Mrs. Wayne Chapman, So-
lana Beach, CA*

Multiple-strand bridal necklace.
*Collection, Mr. & Mrs. Wayne Chapman, So-
lana Beach, CA*

Bridal necklace, Algeria. With silver, coral
beads and gemstones.
*Courtesy, Field Museum of Natural History,
Chicago*

3
Flat
Metalwork

Expert jewelers are abundant in the big cities of Morocco, Pakistan, Afghanistan, Ethiopia, Thailand, India and other countries. They create the objects worn by the people and, more recently, for export. In the North African countries, jewelry remains essentially Moorish in character; in the Asian countries it has an Oriental flavor. The same linear designs that appeared in antique jewelry are often repeated and provide the craftsmen with a wealth of inspiration for traditional and modern pieces. Essentially most pieces have the same motifs as the old, with minor variations. Silver, rather than gold, is more generally suited to life under the dark skies of the deserts and back countries and beside campfires. Shining large and small pendants, heavy bracelets and small silver beads with large amber pieces are as much signs of the peoples as are their clothing and habits.

For the purpose of study and organization, the objects that follow rely on flat shapes rather than the dimensional forms discussed in the previous chapter. Actually it is difficult, perhaps arbitrary, to divorce the flat from the dimensional because many combinations are used in stringing together myriad pieces for necklaces, forehead pieces, earrings, fibulae and other adornments. Yet this quality of variety makes observation so provocative.

During an initial perusal of the examples, you may wish to concentrate on the flatness of the pieces as a solution to design from the jeweler's viewpoint. On the second look, you may wish to concentrate on the types of chains used, or the findings that connect the parts. Then observe how the parts are combined, round with square, flat with dimensional, triangle with the tubular and so forth.

Another observation might be the extensive use of flat coins in the jewelry. Coins are almost everywhere from the souks of North Africa through Central and South America and throughout Asia. When one observes the countless numbers of coins used in the jewelry one wonders, "What is left to be used for money?" Sometimes the jewelry itself is the barter item and the trade object. The craftsmanship may make the object more valuable than the coins

Opposite:
Fatima Hands. Morocco. Throughout the Moslem countries the hand is a symbol that wards off the evil eye and brings good luck. In early Christian art when the countenance of God was not used, the hand symbolized His presence.
Collection, Helen Banes, Silver Spring, MD

Gold bracteate, decorated, eighth century A.D. Flat ornaments of the Vikings were based on designs from Roman coins, but used geometry rather than human figures.
Collection, Museum of National Antiquities, Stockholm

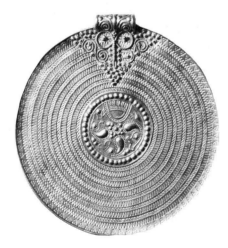

Silver coins, flat rings, and flat fibulae are worn in profusion by a Kalyle woman of Algeria. A Fatima hand hangs from one side of the headpiece. 1934. The jewelry is worn over the head wrap.
Courtesy, Field Museum of Natural History, Chicago

Jewelry motifs, Pakistan, repeat designs in the stone sculpture, fabric, and other arts of the country.

by themselves. Antique coins, used in neckware handed down from mother to daughter, also increase the value.

In native marketplaces, coins from many countries can be purchased easily. These are not necessarily collectors' coins; they are available for any purpose the user chooses. If one needs silver coins the same size, shape and design, they can be bought from baskets full of them. When I was in Peru I was able to purchase enough copper coins of one size and from one country to make an entire necklace. The coins were not Peruvian. I simply selected the ones I wanted. They probably have little or no purchase value anywhere.

In many countries, the artisans melt down silver coins to make other objects. The Tuareg society in the Aïr region of the south-central Sahara make incredible silver figurines from melted coins. The objects reflect the activities of the people—a rider on a silver camel, or implements and utensils. The objects, made for and collected by the wealthy Tuaregs, are created by a group within the society called the Inadan, who live in Talat. Their role is to contrib-

An Afghanistan headshawl has the jewelry pinned or sewn directly to it, and it becomes a forehead adornment. Flat shi sha mirrors in round coinlike shapes are considered jewelry that reflects and adds color to the costumes. They are embroidered onto the bodice, which is trimmed with beadwork.
Courtesy, Folkwear
Photo, Jerry Wainright

Flat coins, combined with beads, are attached to combs and thrust into the piled-up hairdo of a woman of northern Thailand.

ute beauty to the austere desert environment. These skilled Inadan craftsmen are well respected, though of a lower caste than the Tuareg nobles for whom they make the objects.

Jewelry made by the Inadan is seldom the shape of coins themselves; they are more likely flat diamond-shaped pieces, stylized crosses, in long and short tubular beads and in many other shapes. Iron is also used. The pieces are combined with glass and bone beads. Some of the jewelry is made of carved soapstone. The Tuaregs may pay for the pieces in money, a favor or other form of barter.

Compare the pieces that follow and observe the repeat use of basic design elements from the various countries: circles, rectangles, stars, diamonds. Observe the use of stones in simple settings whether the stone is in the center of a fatima hand or in a pendant that hangs on the chest, from a fibula or on a forehead chain. Usually the stones are rounded or flat; they are rarely cut into faceted shapes. They may be agate, carnelian, cinnabar, lapis

Coins are worn on a necklace by a Guatemalan woman working in the marketplace.
She wears it with a bead necklace and
earrings.
Photo, Mel Meilach

Silver coins and silver beads from Guatemala
are strung with small coral beads for spacing.
The coins used are not always Guatemalan;
some may be from other countries.
Collection, Dona Meilach

lazuli or stones native to an area. Coral is used in some of the
pieces. Stones not native to an area are usually obtained by trade.
Where stones are not used, domed pieces of silver may be formed
to simulate a stone and give the raised dimension.

Repoussé, chasing and engraving are the basic techniques used.
Color is often added by enameling, especially in the pieces from
Morocco, or by cloisonné. Twisted wire, granulation and shot are
added to achieve textures.

Large necklaces with many elements from Thailand and nearby
countries often served multiple purposes. Sometimes they were
worn as jewelry; when not worn they may have been hung and
used as wind chimes. Careful observation will show that some of
the dangling pieces are utilitarian objects such as tweezers, ear
spoons, picks and other grooming items, and utensils used for
working with opium.

Coins combined with other jewelry forms are worn by people from the Baltic countries.

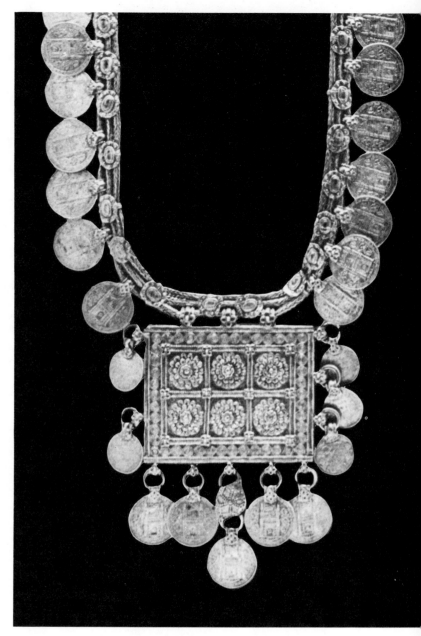

A silver necklace with coins, from Pakistan, is worn by a bridegroom.

The Bedouin woman of North Africa keeps her face shielded from the sand and sun, but her garments are resplendent with coins and silver jewelry in diamond shapes and with colorful tassels made of cotton, silk and rayon.

Opposite:
The shapes of the gold jewelry worn by the Cuna Indians of the San Blas Islands of Central America are unique and very different from those worn by the peoples of other areas. The large earrings, nose rings and beaded bracelets are not so far removed in concept from the tribal jewelry of other cultures thousands of miles away.
Photo, courtesy, Ann Parker, from Molas, Folk Art of the Cuna Indians, *Clarkson N. Potter, Inc.*

Flat jewelry elements made by the people of northern Thailand exhibit the same motifs used over and over, yet with infinite variety. Fish, butterflies, birds, squirrels and leaves are obvious in all the silver shapes. They are repeated as etched designs within other shapes. It is interesting to observe the similarities, with individual differences, in the repeat motifs of the imagery indigenous to the society.
Photographed at Chiang Mai

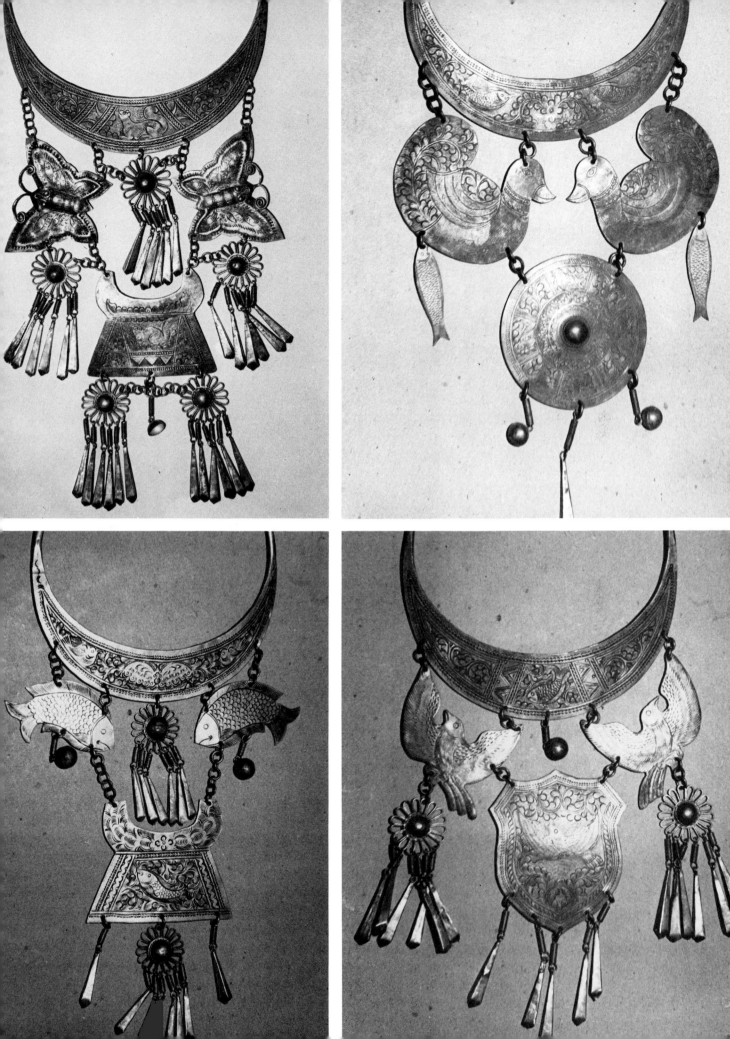

Coils of flat wire hooked within one another are used as links to hold a flat pendant. Northern Thailand.

Rectangular pieces of different sizes are a variation of the shapes on the previous page, with intricate chased designs combined in graduated sizes.

A cast pectoral (chest ornament) is flat with low relief with lizards, a symbol often used in jewelry from Colombia, South America.
Courtesy, Field Museum of Natural History, Chicago

Silver pendants (or what we think of as pendants) from northern Thailand were sometimes used for wind chimes. Observe that the stylized butterfly in the top flat segment has openwork wire floral motifs used as a link between the chain and the dangling flat elements.

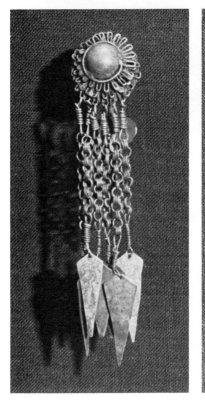

Earrings of northern Thailand repeat the shapes in the neckwear; the endings that clip onto or through the ear are the same stylized elephants often used on necklace clasps.

All northern Thailand jewelry photographed in Thailand by the author

Silver pieces incorporated into pendants were often used as weights for grain or opium by people from Tibet, China and Thailand (see pages 61–62). The arched-back curled animal forms on the pendant represent elephants with their trunks upward to signify good luck. Observe the coiled wire links and the triangular dangling pieces, which are more detailed and more complex than the thin silver flat, bent and crimped shapes in the necklaces on pages 56 to 58.

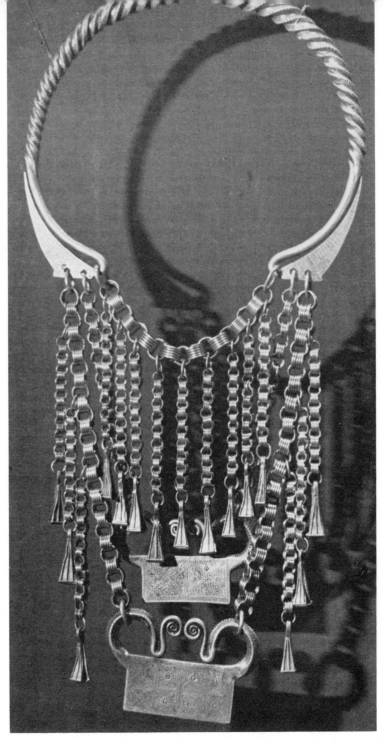

Jewelry with flat and dimensional elements may also be used as wind chimes. The centermost pieces at the bottom are utilitarian objects used for grooming, or for working with opium. The round form at the top is a Buddhist "wheel of law."

Chains and flat pendants with squared designs represent another aspect of Thai design in addition to stylized birds and fish. The arrangement of the chains and the twisted forged neckband suggest that these pieces are older than the flat silver neckband and elements in those on pages 56 and 57.
All jewelry photographed in Thailand by the author

Utilitarian neckpieces contain a variety of tools. Such jewelry often hooked onto other neckwear. Spoons and sharp-pointed utensils were used for opium; others were used for grooming the fingernails or cleaning the ears. The piece above may have been used for measuring powders. The concept of functional objects in a necklace is one that contemporary craftsmen have overlooked.

Photographed at Chiang Mai, Thailand

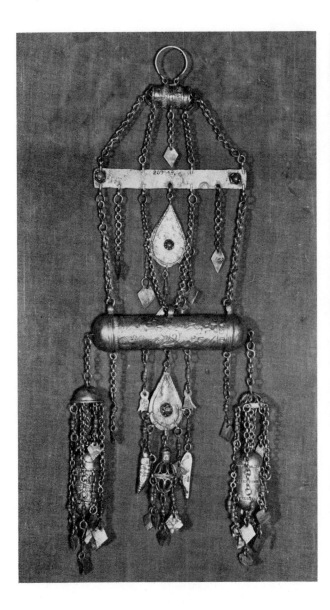

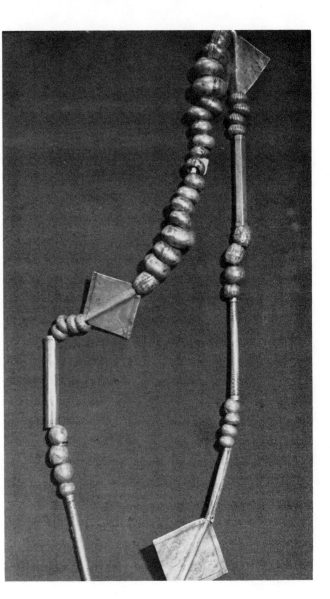

Upper left:
A flat bar and teardrop shapes are combined with a dimensional prayer holder and domed and beaded elements. From Algeria.
Courtesy, Field Museum of Natural History, Chicago

Above:
Combinations of flat shapes, tubes and beads appear on a necklace from Northern Asia.

Left:
A Tuareg woman in the southern Sahara desert wears intricately shaped, beautifully hammered and cast silver jewelry made by the Inadans, the artisans within the society. Silver glass beads and embroidery help to decorate the drab stark monotony of the Sahara existence for the Tuaregs. Beads are used in necklaces as well as strung on long hair as "hair beads."

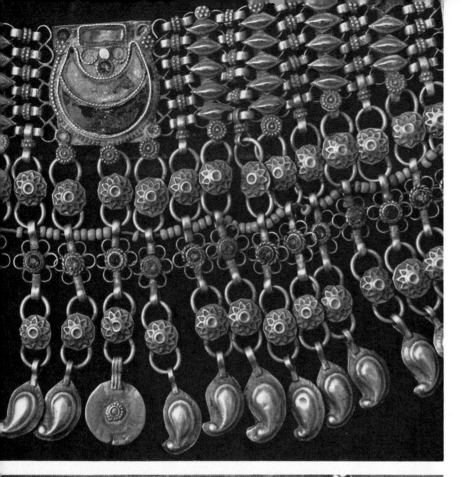

Incredible details and combinations of multiple small elements are repeated in a collar-like necklace probably from Persia. The Islamic crescent moon is in the top center; solid stamped rosettes, glass beads and wire rosettes are linked in the central position. The ancient Persian paisley motif is on the raised forms of each drop ending. A flat coinlike piece is in the center.
Collection, Helen Banes, Silver Spring, MD

A jewelry "apron" is worn over a silk printed skirt. Varying shapes of flattened silver are combined with strands of beads. Many of the designs on the silver shapes are composed of ritual figures.
Collection, Field Museum of Natural History, Chicago

Rosettes in a necklace from Pakistan are made with open wirework and some stamped repeats for connecting links.

Detail of a necklace from Rajasthan, India. The pieces are interlinked in such a way that they have the feeling of being "hinged." *Collection, Mr. & Mrs. Wayne Chapman, Solana Beach, CA*

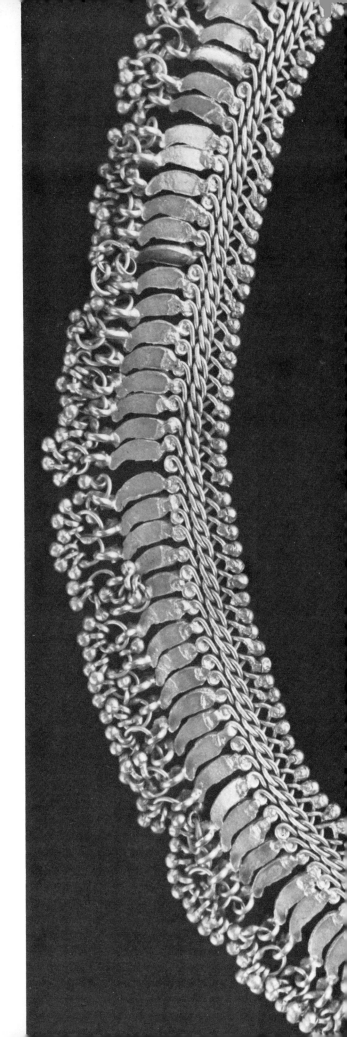

As in most ethnic cultures, the Tibetan natives wear many strands of different kinds of jewelry as a total body ornamentation. Observe how the functional piece of jewelry, with the grooming tools, a brush, pick and spoon, is suspended from one side of the beaded necklace; it is not worn around the neck.

A flat silver pendant, lightly punched for the dot design, has, in the bezel, a semiprecious white carnelian stone believed to ward off the evil eye. The two tiny silver shapes at the bottom are stylized fish, called botas, of Persian origin. The pendant is strung with large silver beads banded with twisted silver wire, smaller round and flat silver beads and amber. Turkoman, southern Russia.

Collection, Peterson Conway & Sons, Carmel Valley, CA

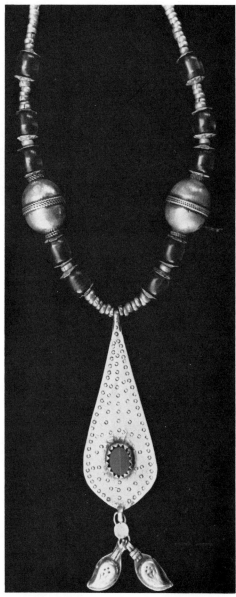

A flat collar torque necklace with a chased floral design and the typical Cambodian elephant trunk closure, from Cambodia. Coiled wire and formed metal endings are similar to those on Thai necklaces, but the silver is heavier and the endings are added to the torque portion; it does not have the separate parts assembled as do the Thai pieces.

Collection, Mr. & Mrs. Wayne Chapman, Solana Beach, CA

A contemporary Israeli necklace is made of an etched and enameled flat ring and bars.
Private Collection

A wedding collar from southern Asia. The flat band is set with stones and circles that repeat the elements holding the dangling portions. The endings are symbolic of the penis.
Courtesy, Peterson Conway & Sons, Carmel Valley, CA

Calligraphy, real and stylized, is frequently used for design in jewelry from many cultures.

Left and above:
From Israel.

Opposite, top left:
From Israel.

Opposite, top right:
Priest's necklace with a Koranic inscription and the bota fish symbol repeated on the pendant and the small beads. Afghanistan or Iran.

Opposite, below:
Earrings, Israel.

The cross, made in infinite variations since the beginning of Christianity, and even before, reflects the style of the area in which it has been created. A distinct cross design is that of the Yalalags of Mexico near Oaxaca. Usually a large cross form is the dominant element from which smaller crosses are suspended. The ball-shaped bead represents the pomegranate, a basic Christian symbol with varying symbolism. Primarily, it represents the church because of the inner unity of countless seeds in one and the same fruit. It additionally symbolizes fertility because of its many seeds, and of the hope for immortality and resurrection. The crosses (*above and opposite, left*) are by the Yalalags.
Collection, Casa de Pancho, San Diego, CA

Typical cast silver charms from Mexico. *Top to bottom:* A prayer is written on the charm; a male figure; the foot symbolizes humility and servitude because it touches the ground; the fish represents Christ and baptism.
Collection, Casa de Pancho, San Diego, CA

Above:
Contemporary designs from Africa are essentially flat with repoussé low relief areas.
Private Collection

Above, right:
Cast gold piece from the Tairona culture, Colombia, about A.D. 1000. This beautiful piece illustrates the dress of warriors of the period.
Collection, Susan Nelson, Palos Verdes Estates, CA

Right:
Cast gold pendant from Peru with figures and mask.
Private Collection

Opposite:
A silver pendant from Bali shows the Ramayan Demon holding an antique Chinese bronze coin.
Private collection

4
Openwork and Inlay

Openwork is an often-used jewelry design concept. The resulting negative spaces within are an important element and may or may not repeat the form of the piece itself.

Most openwork pieces are the result of piercing. Portions are removed from a flat sheet of metal with a jeweler's saw or by drilling holes or punching out shapes. An openwork object may also be created by the lost-wax casting process.

Filigree is an openwork technique that has the appearance of lace. Filigree designs differ by country, but the methods remain essentially the same. Soft annealed flat, braided or twisted wire is shaped into units. The design may be a coil, oval, fan, spiral, scroll, comma, shell or other form. The units are then soldered together to make the total arrangement. Spaces may be filled with finer wires or with round shot.

Filigree is often found in jewelry from Mexico, India, Israel, Greece and many Eastern countries. It is also used as decoration on utensils and on objects such as purses, mirrors and boxes.

In Morocco and other African countries, the filigree look is not always true openwork; rather, it is wire made to look like filigree. Thin lacy wire designs are placed on a metal backing. The result is an open look, but it is not see-through.

Openwork silver beads that you can observe in many necklaces are made by an assembly technique. A bead is actually made of two domed parts separated by one or more strips of metal. These have been cut into a wavy line, a zigzag or a strip with circle or diamond shapes pierced out. The strip is simply soldered between both halves of the dome to result in a bead with a partially open center element.

In some beads, the flat piece of metal may be punched, then shaped into a tube with a cap fitted on each end to create a long, narrow openwork bead. Such beads were often used as hair holders for long braids. Openwork pieces, lighter weight than solid jewelry forms, are popular in India, Sikkim, Cambodia and areas of Nepal for nose rings and earrings; but they appear in other jewelry, too.

Opposite:
Frequently, one can identify the country of origin of a jewelry item by knowing and recognizing the motifs used in other decorative arts. A necklace worn by a Moroccan woman repeats the designs found in embroidery, appliqué, wood and tile work of Morocco.

The Japanese symbol suggests the origin of the silver pendant. The openwork is made by cutting areas away with a jeweler's saw.

An ancient Roman necklace has openwork
pendants and long beads with fluted endings.
Coins are set within the pendants. The pieces
are strung on a chain with V-shaped links.
*Courtesy, Field Museum of Natural History,
Chicago*

A Moroccan gypsy wears openwork earrings
suspended from a round ball. Several chain
and coin necklaces dangle around her neck.

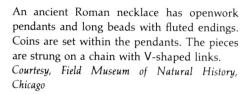

Openwork and solid portions of many of the jewels illustrated in
this chapter are combined with cabochon or flat settings of large
gemstones or nuggets such as tourmaline, carnelian, turquoise, amber, topaz, rubies and pearls.

Observe, too, the textures of the elements: Some may combine
shiny and matte surfaces; others may be all shiny or all matte. The
use of metals with gemstones provides color as well as textural
change. The combinations of metals with glass or ceramic always
give vitality and variety to jewelry.

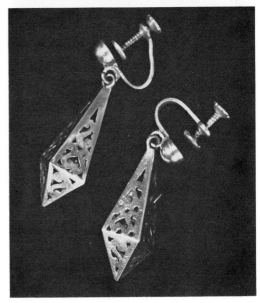

Above, left:
An antique flat openwork silver pendant, China. The etched design on each side is different.
Collection, Lee Erlin Snow, Los Angeles, CA

Above, right:
A fibula consists of a pendant with openwork wire and pierced beads with some gemstones. The hooked finding at the top is used to suspend the piece from another strand of beads. Algeria.
Courtesy, Field Museum of Natural History, Chicago

Designs are stamped out of sheets of silver which are then bent, fabricated and soldered to make attractive earrings. Mexico.
Collection, Dona Meilach

Jewelry from Algeria illustrates openwork elements probably made by the casting process. The closure is on one side rather than at the center back. A variety of hands, fish, links and beads are arranged symmetrically.
Courtesy, Field Museum of Natural History, Chicago

The same openwork used in jewelry is emulated in a Balinese leather shadow puppet. The placement of jewelry and the designs are evident in the headpiece, necklace, chest and belt adornments, armbands and bracelets, which are all combined in the costumes worn by dancers, too.

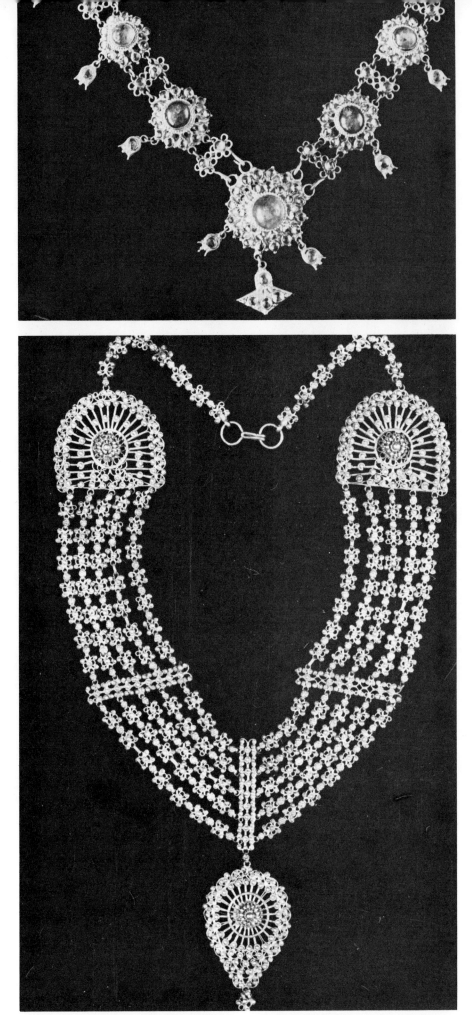

A contemporary design of cast gold openwork from Thailand with gemstones. The piece interprets traditional Thai jewelry designs.
Collection, Nangyo Karnchan-achari, Bangkok, Thailand

An openwork necklace with jewels. Algeria.
Courtesy, Field Museum of Natural History, Chicago

Opposite, far left:
Crescent and round shapes in openwork brass
and silver. Some gemstones. Morocco.

Opposite, left:
Portion of a fibula with pendants, bells and
other charms; cast and pierced. Algeria.

Ancient gold collar, hammered and forged and
assembled. Peru.
Private collection

Gemstones are set in gold in one of a pair of ancient large Etruscan earrings. There is granulation within the design and ball shapes with beads around the edge.
Courtesy, Field Museum of Natural History, Chicago

Precious and semiprecious stones are an integral part of ethnic jewelry in countries where the stones are available or traded. A Tibetan belt buckle is set with a polished brown tourmaline stone.
Collection, Mr. & Mrs. Wayne Chapman, Solana Beach, CA

Drawing for a costume for "Le Dieu Bleu," a dance performance in the 1920s. Costumes designed for stage productions illustrate how the jewelry may be worn on the head, neck, arms and navel. By Leon Bakst.

An ornate ankle bracelet from India is composed of rubies and pearls set in silver. Sometimes anklets, worn one on top of the other, reached halfway up the leg.

Courtesy, Field Museum of Natural History, Chicago

Multiple bezels hold stones in star shapes that repeat the form of the flat silver-chased disc with a scalloped edge. The pendant may be worn from a large fibula on the forehead. Morocco.

A pierced pendant with gemstones is worn as a forehead adornment by a woman of Morocco. The coin necklace is strung on thick multiples of yarn strands; the fibula holds her cape together.

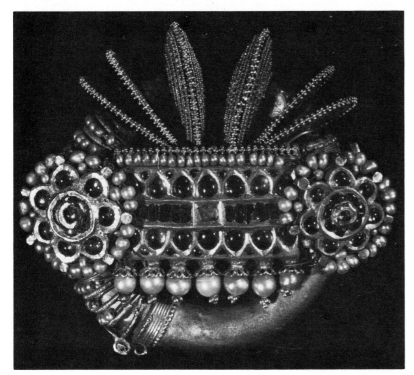

A bib-like collar necklace made of silver with gemstones and twisted wire elements. Large collars may be worn low on the chest as shown in the costume of the young Morrocan girl *(left)*. The placement of the pieces so close to one another results in a pattern of negative space.

Opposite:
Necklaces from the Bedouin tribes of Afghanistan are silver with carnelian and other colored gemstones.
Collection, Helen Banes, Silver Spring, MD

Grand fibula from Morocco *(right)* illustrates a variety of jewelry techniques: piercing, stone setting, repoussé, chasing and assembling. Note the use of the fibula *(above)*, one at each shoulder, to hold a portion of a garment in place.

Opposite:
A belt, probably worn by royalty in the eighteenth century, is from Bukhara, southern Russia. It combines silver with niello work, and the silver rounds are stitched to the woven fabric. Sealed prayers were probably placed on rice paper under the silver.

Collection, Peterson Conway & Sons, Carmel Valley, CA

An elegant dowry necklace probably passed on from generation to generation by the Kazakh tribeswomen of Russia. Stones of coral and cherry amber are combined with hand-wrought silver filigree beads and silver settings.
Collection, Peterson Conway & Sons, Carmel Valley, CA

Right: Detail.

Gold and silver pierced and wire jewelry with agates and stones are an integral part of the Balinese dancers' costumes. Some pendants are stitched directly to the fabric collar. Designs of the jewelry are repeated in the silver-and-gold thread stitching on the fabric.
Photographed in Bali by the authors

Design elements in jewelry, sculpture and other art forms are shared by many countries. The large silver circular bead in a Mexican necklace is very much like the rosette in a stone carving from India *(right)*.

Metalwork hinges and decorative portions of a box and the carving on the woodwork have counterparts in the jewelry and fabric of the Orient.
Private collection

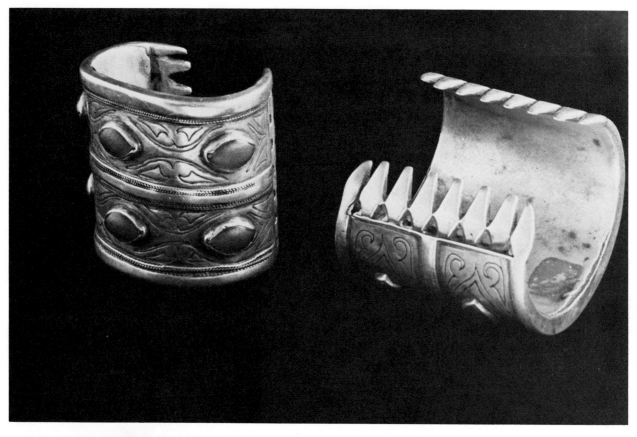

BRACELETS, CUFFS, RINGS

Bracelets, or cuffs, as they are sometimes called, are an essential piece of jewelry in many ethnic cultures. Bracelets of different styles and from many countries and rings for the nose, fingers and ears are shown. Archers' rings from China are often of a pierced silver or of carved jade with various types of inlay and enamel work combined. All the pieces shown are but a tiny sampling of the types and quantity of examples available from any one country. They may give you clues to identifying your own jewelry as to origin and technique. A study of the various types and styles will lead to an appreciation of the infinite variety that exists in jewelry from around the world.

Above, a pair of silver Turkoman bracelets set with carnelian stones from central Asia. A bracelet such as this might be ancient and in a museum. The same type of jewelry continues to be worn today in Soviet and Afghan Turkestan. Sometimes the stones are glass lozenges.
Collection, Mr. & Mrs. Wayne Chapman, Solana Beach, CA

Left:
Our ever-present camera in a native marketplace in Zagora, southern Morocco, revealed the typical bracelet, and the heavy earrings, worn with a hand-embroidered shawl by a woman going about her shopping.

A silver cuff from Thailand has an interplay of solid silver chased detailing. The silver "mesh" is intricately pierced to yield the appearance of knitting.

A contemporary bracelet from Israel has a faceted stone suspended within the negative area.
Private Collection

A contemporary bracelet from Israel assembled with various teardrop and oval silver domes.
Private collection

A wide Algerian cuff has a variety of shaped designs made with stamping tools and combined with gemstones and metal domes above and below.
Courtesy, Field Museum of Natural History, Chicago

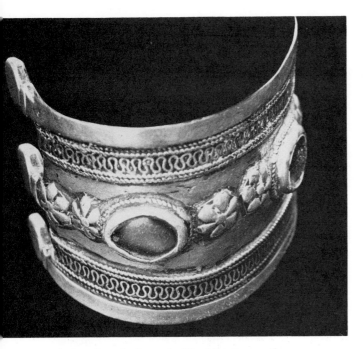

A silver bracelet from the Kazakh tribe, southern Russia, with a crystal gemstone.
Private collection

Opposite:
Three bracelets made of chased silver. The silver band is wrapped around a circle of bamboo. China.
Photographed at the Gallery of Oriental Antiques, Palos Verdes Estates, CA

A more intricately designed bracelet with a carved stone face and the stones made into a figure is also from the Meo hill tribe of northern Thailand. The grooved edge of the curved wires placed on a background give the effect of filigree.

A silver bracelet with domes that follow the familiar rosette design. Northern Thailand, Meo tribe.

A Berber silver bracelet with stones set rather crudely in various silver bezels. Some have dropped off, which suggests that all the pieces are not of the same quality craftsmanship.
Collection, Marie-Dominguez Ferre, Paris

A variety of rings from different countries for fingers, ears and nose:

1. From Israel, the circle repeat using twisted wire, coiled wire and shot.

2. Ancient finger ring. Roman.
Courtesy, Field Museum of Natural History, Chicago

3. Cast gold ring with beads that support a carved black stone. Etruscan.
Courtesy, Field Museum of Natural History, Chicago

4 and 5. Cast silver rings. China.

6 and 7. Archers' rings. China. The ring is worn on the thumb to protect the thumb from the string of the bow. Repoussé. Some archers' rings are made of jade.
Collection, Gallery of Oriental Antiques, Palos Verdes Estates, CA

8. One of a pair of earrings from Greece. Gold. Shaped and forged.

9. One of a pair of silver earrings from Mycenae. Triangular shaped and covered with shot.

10. One of a pair of Etruscan earrings in silver with domes and shot.

Gold nose ring with gemstones. India.
*Photo courtesy, Field Museum of Natural History,
Chicago*

Hand ornament, India. Five rings connected
by gold chains. Some enameling within the
silver leaf shapes. The larger areas are set with
rock crystals and rubies. One ring has a large
setting and, because of its end position, is
probably worn on the thumb. The large me-
dallions are placed on the wrist and back of
the hand as shown in the hand ornament
(right) from Pakistan.
Private Collection

A craftsman in Kyoto, Japan, taps gold and silver leaf into the intricately chiseled outlines of steel bars. The bars are secured on a bed of pitch to prevent them from slipping as they are worked.

Japanese Damascene work involves chiseling very fine crosshatch lines in a steel plate with precision-sharp instruments. Silver and gold leaf are tapped into the lines in the given design arrangement. The surface of the steel is corroded with nitric acid and rusted to yield a dark background that will set off the gold and silver visually. Rusting is stopped by placing the bar in boiling green tea. Then the gold and silver are polished out with soft charcoal. Final engraving and polishing are accomplished.

THE ART OF INLAY

Inlay is among the universal techniques used in jewelry making, and it can involve the use of many different materials placed one in another. The technique, with variations, may appear in jewelry made by different cultures and called by other names.

Inlay may involve placing one metal within another or placing a strand of silver wire in another material such as wood. Niello work is a form of metal on metal decoration that contrasts a base metal color with a black metal alloy. "Niello" is the Italian form of the Latin word *nigellum,* meaning black. It was used by ancient Egyptians, Greeks, Romans and Persians and is still used in the Far East, especially in Thailand, where it is called "Krueng tome." Niello work has also been used extensively for sword handles, gun handles and other weaponry objects.

"Damascene" work refers to the process of inlaying gold or silver wire into bronze, iron or steel. It was practiced in ancient China and Egypt, then in Damascus, from which the name "Damascene" work evolved. Many forms of Damascene work spread throughout the Eastern and Asian cultures; today it is practiced to a fine degree by Japanese craftsmen of Kyoto. Designs are engraved and etched into a base metal; gold leaf is hammered into the engraved line, then smoothed so the surface is perfectly flat.

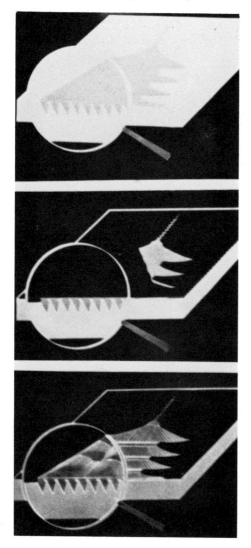

Finished Damascene pendants. Kyoto, Japan.

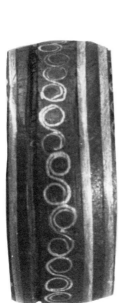

Silver wire inlaid in an ebony wood bracelet. Egypt.
Collection, Mme. Werner Bocqué, Brussels, Belgium

Damascene pendants with shadings of silver
and gold leaf. Kyoto, Japan.
*Photographed at the Amita Handcraft Center,
Kyoto, Japan*

Ebony wood beads inlaid with silver wire are combined with silver pendants. India.
Collection, Helen Banes, Silver Spring, MD

Cloisonné bead. Mexico.

Enameling on metal has many variations. Techniques originated in ancient times are still practiced by contemporary craftsmen throughout the world.

The art of enameling consists of applying a thin coat of glass to certain metals, then firing both the metal and glass to a red-hot heat. The glass melts and fuses to the metal. This is called "painted enamel." Other enameling-on-metal techniques are:

CLOISONNÉ	Thin wires are shaped along the backing metal and used to separate the colors. Glass particles are placed between the *cloisons* (meaning cells) and melted.
CHAMPLEVÉ	Differs from *cloisonné*. In *champlevé,* the areas that receive enamel are either etched or carved away, enabling the metal to show in some areas.

PLIQUE-À-JOUR Gives the effect of stained glass. The enamel is translucent as there is no metal backing where the enamel is fused together.

GRISAILLE Is an effect of light and shade produced in painted enamels. The background is covered with an opaque white and modulated to produce gradations of light and shade.

Above:
Ebony wood is inlaid with wide and narrow silver wire in a bracelet from Egypt.
Collection, Mme. Werner Bocqué, Brussels, Belgium

Right:
Cloisonné beads at the top, and a painted enamel and cloisonné pendant, bottom.
Collection, Mr. & Mrs. Wayne Chapman, Solana Beach, CA

101

Champlevé enamel pendant. India. The silver wire is raised with the predominately blue and red enamel designs melted low in the pockets formed by the silver.
Collection, Lee Erlin Snow, Los Angeles, CA

A cloisonné pendant is suspended from multiple chains with additional pendants on each side near the neck. Pakistan.

Opposite:
Straight silver wire and slices of shaped silver wire are laid on a metal backing. The resulting spaces are filled in with blue enamel in a form of cloisonné. The pendant is strung on a chain of silver beads with rare lemon amber beads. Southern Russia, about 1800.
Collection, Dona Meilach

5
Stones—
Plain and Carved

Gemstones, rocks and minerals are integral components of jewelry. The materials used by any and every culture depend on availability and on what is revered and considered precious. In Western societies, diamonds, rubies, pearls and similar gems are desired for their beauty.

In many ethnic societies, the precious and semiprecious stones used vary. Perhaps among the more dramatic, and romantic, stones to the Western eye are the large and small opaque amber beads. In the desert countries of Morocco and Afghanistan and in the coastal areas of Africa, women are often pictured with strings of amber beads worn simultaneously with multiple strands of silver, glass and sometimes fiber jewelry. The beautiful, smooth amber beads range in color tones and in size from small, flat washer shapes to some that are as large and round as peaches.

Possession of beads is a symbol of status and represents a husband's ability as a provider. I sometimes think a wealthy husband would be a burden as the beads are extremely heavy. I marveled at how women could wear them for long periods of time. For they are worn often and not brought out only for special occasions. Bedouin groups must carry their wealth with them, and the women look magnificent riding on camels or donkeys or sitting at their weaving looms with the beautiful amber about their chests.

When amber is mentioned, most people think of Baltic amber, a transparent hard stone in ranges of pale yellow to black and from which the word "amber" derives its name as a color. The more valuable amber pieces may contain tiny fossilized pieces of trees or bugs. Often these bugs are from another geological period and they no longer exist within nature today. The presence of such fossils makes the pieces extremely valuable for study and collection. Sea amber is usually found along the shores of England, Denmark, Sweden and the Prussian Baltic coast. Some of it is mined from pits in Baltic locations.

Opaque amber, favored by African groups, is a particular form of tree resin or sap that was buried and pressed beneath the earth during great changes in the earth's surface millions of years ago, probably during Oligocene times. As the amber sap exuded from

Opposite:
Amber beads signify wealth in African cultures. The beads, in magnificent yellow-gold colors and subtle shadings, are fashioned in a variety of sizes and shapes. Strands may consist of amber beads only, or the beads may be interspersed with silver pieces.
Collection, Dona Meilach

A polished piece of walrus ivory is the setting for a metal "menuki," a small decoration usually found on a Japanese samurai sword handle. A metal ojimi bead is at the top.
Collection, Mr. & Mrs. Wayne Chapman, Solana Beach, CA

Amber in various sizes, shapes and shades of coloring is combined in any number of ways with other beads of stone and silver in necklaces photographed in Morocco.

A young girl from Aït Haddiddou, near Marrakesh, southern Morocco, wears two strands of amber beads with her silver-laden headdress.

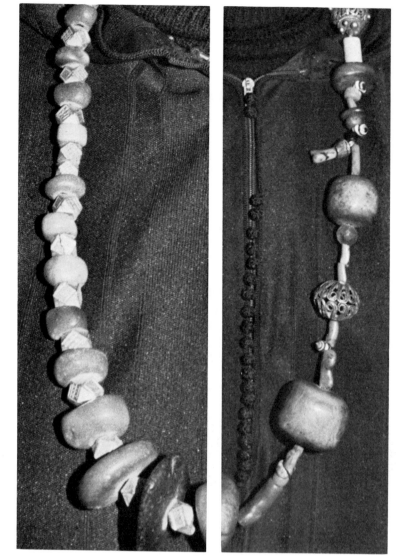

the trees, many natural phenomena acted upon the material to result in infinite variety and beauty. Bubbles, long cracks of another color, mottling, and tones of color with streaks of red, dark reddish brown and light yellows resulted from varying layers of sap running together, air trapped within the sap, the presence of certain chemicals and other factors.

Today, tree amber is usually found in lumps beneath the earth and in a semi-fossilized condition, primarily in Mozambique, Somalia and the coastal area of Zanzibar. You will see references to copal amber, which is of great interest to the ethnic culture. The word "copal" is derived from a Central American Indian word "copalli," which probably means "resin."

Africans have their own names for the materials that are brought up from shallow digs only three or four feet into the ground where no trees grow today. In Zanzibar, amber is called "Sandarusi" if it is the semi-fossilized variety. A raw material obtained from the sap of a living tree is termed "animi" or "chakazi." Raw copal, which is not as hard as is semi-fossilized copal, is exported to other countries to be used in the manufacture of varnish.

Somali amber beads with silver. Somali amber is soapier, more irregular and lighter in weight than copal amber. A string of the beads in different sizes is combined with Ethiopian silver beads.
Collection, Mrs. & Mrs. Wayne Chapman, Solana Beach, CA

The term "copal" is applied to many resins that vary in appearance, age, constitution, source and texture. Some are soapier and lighter weight than others; some are more porous and will result in different surface textures. Preference is a matter of taste.

Sorting out the names and types of ambers is difficult, and even the literature in encyclopedias, gemology books and bead articles is filled with "maybe's," "if's," and "probably's." When components of jewelry are labeled, you will note that there are many different ambers. The material is usually named for the country of origin so that:

Burmite is amber from Burma
Rumanite is amber of Rumania
Simetite is amber from Sicily

Through the years, ambers have been credited by various cultures with having curative, medical and mystical properties. Not too long ago, beautiful opaque ambers were used as a unit of trade by tribes in the region of the upper Volta River and could be bartered for a bride. One large bead was equivalent to four cows; a smaller bead may have been equivalent to two cows.

Those who wish to collect amber are cautioned to study the material carefully because it has been imitated in plastic, which, by appearance, is an incredible replica of the real thing. If you plan to purchase amber as an investment, learn the differences between the types of amber, where they come from, by look, by feel, by density and by chemical analysis, if necessary.

Ivory from elephant tusks and walrus tusks and the teeth of other large mammals is made into beads by many cultures. The Japanese carve ivory ojimi beads, used on their netsukes. They are valued by collectors, and one bead can cost hundreds of dollars.

Jade, malachite, ruby, carnelian, turquoise, agate, coral that is rough and highly polished, are all used in beads from various cultures. Most are rounded or flat rather than cut and faceted; it seems the preference is to leave the stone in as natural a state as possible.

The oval metal pieces are "fushi," the guards at the top of a Japanese sword handle. Barbara Chapman combined two fushi as one bead. They were strung together with an amber and turquoise bead above the fushi and a Mexican malachite bead below it. At the bottom are a silver Persian bead and a brown jade stone carved in the form of a cicada. In ancient Chinese tombs, carved cicadas were placed on the tongues of the dead to enable them to chatter in heaven.

Carved ivory ojimi beads are used as sliders on a netsuke. Japan. They may represent a mask, poetry or stories rather than one-word symbols as in other cultures. Here one can see a carved ivory bell and a sparrow. Silver beads with vertical lines are Japanese.
Collection, Mr. & Mrs. Wayne Chapman, Solana Beach, CA

Ojimi beads, jade rings, pieces of animal vertebra bone, tubular stone, ceramic and silver beads, mostly from Japan, are combined.
Collection, Mr. & Mrs. Wayne Chapman, Solana Beach, CA

Opposite:
Branch coral and polished coral beads, camel bone, round beads and silver beads are used in the wedding collars of the Uzbekistan tribe, southern Russia.
Collection, Helen Banes, Silver Spring, MD

A netsuke bead in the shape of a carp, the fish symbol of Japan.

A carved wooden box, possibly Portuguese, opens and closes and is used as a pendant. A rider on horseback crosses a landscape in the bottom portion of the box. Floral motifs are on the cover.

All details are from necklaces by Barbara Chapman.
Collection, Mr. & Mrs. Wayne Chapman, Solana Beach, CA

An antique jade rabbit and a jade and coral bead are strung on leather. China.

Jade pendant from China with the "skin" on it. This skin covering of the stone is normally polished off, but it has been retained and cut through to yield another color on the raised surface. Various Chinese beads are combined with the jade pendant.

Detail of a necklace with Chinese carved ivory, African carnelian beads and silver pieces from China. The cat (right) is an unusual motif in Chinese beads.

Snake vertebrae, amber and coral, with a face carved in a Japanese jade bead. Below that is a cloisonné bead, an ivory fan holder piece and a carved jade piece. From a necklace by Barbara Chapman.
Collection, Mr. & Mrs. Wayne Chapman, Solana Beach, CA

Soapstone beads in the shapes of heads. Mexico.
Private collection

112

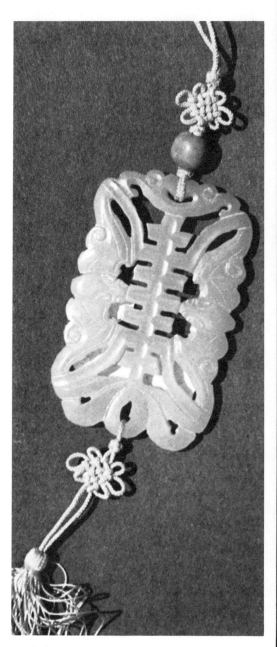

Jade pendant. China.
Collection, The Gallery, Palos Verdes, CA

Jade carvings and jade link chain. K'ien-lung period. China.
Courtesy, Field Museum of Natural History, Chicago

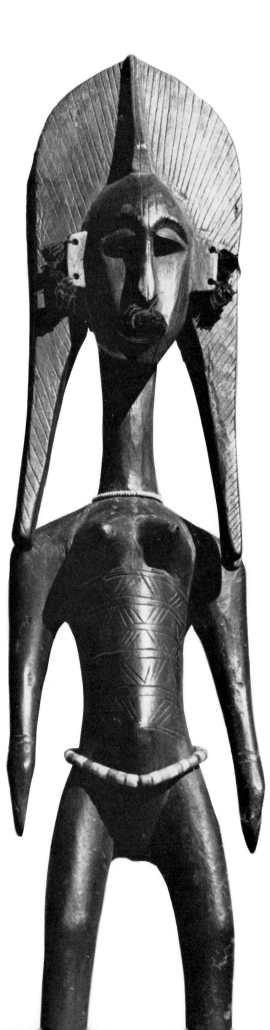

A wooden sculpture of the Bambara tribe, Africa, is adorned with a strand of shell beads at the neck and glass beads at the hip. Fiber tassels through the nose, in the lobes and tops of the ears, and scarification on the body illustrate the various types of adornment worn by the people themselves.
Collection, Dona Meilach

6
Glass, Bones, Shells and Whatnot

The writings by archeologists, ethnologists, historians and other specialists who address their attention to the jewelry of a culture are fascinating and frustrating. One can pore over pages and pages of an article seeking a clue about how a certain bead is used but find information only about a bead's probable age, composition, production and so forth. Even then, there is much conjecture.

The purpose of the following is to offer a display of types of beads and how they have been and still are being used in various cultures. It is not meant to shed new light on unanswered questions raised by specialists. The pieces are selected to share the beauty of the jewelry and to stimulate further study of a culture through this medium. Who knows where the presentation will lead in light of any one person's own interests?

To simplify the presentation, the first part of the chapter deals with glass, wood and ceramics. The next section shows materials gleaned from nature but further fashioned by man's hand to make them wearable. The final section deals with natural materials that do not require much help from man other than slicing, boring a hole, polishing or sorting to make them usable in jewelry. Here you will see an astonishing assortment of shells, teeth, bones, seed, hard fruit, feathers, quills and more.

As with the necklaces in the previous chapters, it is difficult to separate the jewelry into clear-cut divisions by materials. The bead maker will combine many dissimilar materials: There may be bones threaded with silver; glass with feathers; and so forth. Shells, coral, carnelian, bones and silver may all be used in one costume piece.

The seeming lack of organization that defies organization is part of the allure of tribal jewelry from Africa and Asia. It is a concept that is spilling over into the creation of ethnic jewelry by today's urban craftspeople. Several such examples are included in this chapter; there are more in Chapter 7.

Glass beads have appeared all over the world, but those that are known as African trade beads are unusually bright and colorful. Actually, the early African beads were made in Europe; it is believed they were first brought to Africa in the sixteenth century when the European trader realized their exchange value. Beads

A tribesman from Kenya, North Africa, wears strings of beads crossed around his chest and back.

An assortment of Venetian glass beads shows the variation in texture and design. The bead in the third row from the bottom is the millefiore (thousand flowers).

Ceramic beads from Mexico are square, round or tubular and strung with smaller beads and coiled wire on leather strands.

were easily portable, and Africans found the shapes and colors irresistible. Traders commissioned Venetian glassmakers, particularly, to create large quantities and varieties of beads to be used as currency in trading with the Africans.

Venetian beads were originally made by families working in their homes. Molten glass was drawn into long tubes, gathered and cut into sections, or wound around a rod into tubular—or oval—beads. All the techniques used in the intricacies of blowing and forming larger glass pieces produced beads that retained a very high quality.

In the eighteenth century, glassmaking centers evolved in Holland and Czechoslovakia. Different and more varied styles of glass beads resulted and were equally welcomed by the Africans.

The original bead patterns, colors and shapes have become an isolated study area for some specialists. Several museums boast unusual collections of the beads. Articles devoted to African trade beads appear in magazines frequently. Anyone—collector or craftsman—who wishes to delve further into the study of beads could

Sliced horn, sliced and polished stone, sea urchin spines, seashells, carved bone and ivory are used as beads in many societies.

Clay beads from ancient Ecuador were incised and colored with lime or other clays. They depict wild animals and household pets, bats, fish and some plant forms.

begin research with the publications listed in the Bibliography.

Among the trade beads most often found—many are still being made—are the intricately patterned, brilliantly colored millefiore, which means "a thousand flowers." Their manufacture involves a lengthy production procedure, which accounts for their high value and price.

The "eye" motif appears in many beads. It is an ancient symbol associated with the sun and the ability to ward off evil forces. The original eye beads were yellow with a colored dot in the center. Today they can be a red outer layer with a white dot. The dot may appear within a slice of the glass or around the outside of a bead.

Other designs are spirals, chevrons, snake bones, textured beads, fluted shapes and faceted shapes. Long glass beads in the form of hollow cylinders were made by the Dutch in light blue shades.

In each culture throughout Africa, glass beads were given a name in the tribe's language. A blue striped bead was called a "rikiki." A bead with a white core covered with a transparent layer of red glass was known as the "rose bead," "ox eye," or "white heart." One

Wooden beads on display in a South American market illustrate the variety available. Such strands can be cut apart to yield individually shaped and textured beads that may be reassembled in new arrangements.

A four-strand wooden prayer-bead necklace from India. It is used with both hands inside the strands, and each bead is used in turn to say a prayer at the mosque or temple.
Collection, Mrs. Robert Rothschild, Northbrook, IL

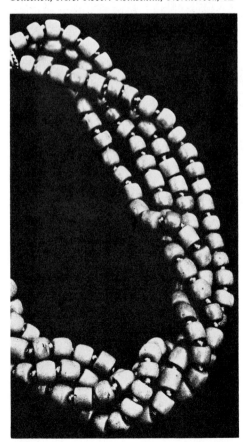

source notes that these beads were worn by elders when grandchildren and great-grandchildren were born.

There is evidence supporting the existence of bead-making centers in India as well as in Europe. In her book, *The Universal Bead*, Jean Mowat Erikson suggests that "glass beads also abound throughout India, and indicate by their type of manufacture, their shape and their color that they were made there. Recent study in Bombay State in the newly excavated old town of Brahmapuri shows that glass must have been made there in very ancient times and that beads similar to those found in quantity in Africa were produced there."

Today, in West Africa, glass beads are made using a soft "powder-glass" as reported by Alastair Lamb in his article titled "Krobo Powder-Glass Beads" (*African Arts Magazine*, April 1976). He discusses Bodom, Krobo, Akosu beads and others and the glass-making procedures in Nigeria and Ghana. He talks about their value and folklore. The article should be read by anyone who wishes to delve further into bead making, beads and their legends. The bead aficionado is also referred to current and past issues of the magazine, *Ornament*, formerly titled *Bead Journal*, for scholarly insights on bead collecting, bead categories, composition and so forth in great depth.

In the 1800s as trade with the Americas evolved, tiny glass seed beads became valued by American Indians. Their bright colors, regularity and availability from traders in exchange for furs made them easier to obtain and more decorative than seeds, teeth, claws

A northern Thailand woman strings tiny beads for use on garments. Observe the elephant endings on her bracelet.

and quills. Some small glass beads, irregularly shaped, were made by the Indians themselves as they sat over open fires.

Indians throughout much of North America were extremely innovative in the use of beads as decoration for clothing. Most of the garments were made from irregularly shaped hides, which were difficult to piece and sew together. The irregular seams could be covered with bands of beaded material, so that sewn beads and woven panels were used extensively. Thus was born the rich heritage of Indian beadwork as we know it today.

As more beads were available, ideas for their application abounded and many can be observed in museum collections. Looms were developed, and recently, similar looms became a popular craft item for re-creating the designs and techniques of long ago. Woven bead panels result in a beaded fabric that can be sewn to another fabric. Single beads and rows of beads can also be strung on a thread and attached directly to a fabric base.

Wood and ceramic beads played a major role in many cultures. Ceramic beads from South American countries and Mexico are an integral part of their artistic development and heritage. Some glazes were used, but essentially the brown and red colors that dominate indicate the types of clay available.

Another ceramic bead associated with ancient and ethnic jewelry is the faience bead. It was first made by Italians at Faenza, from which it received its name. Today the blue faience bead is more often associated with Egyptian jewelry.

A child's hat is adorned with strands of tiny colorful beads; each strand has a coin or bell on the end. Northern Thailand.

Various lengths of seed and shell beads worn by American Indians.

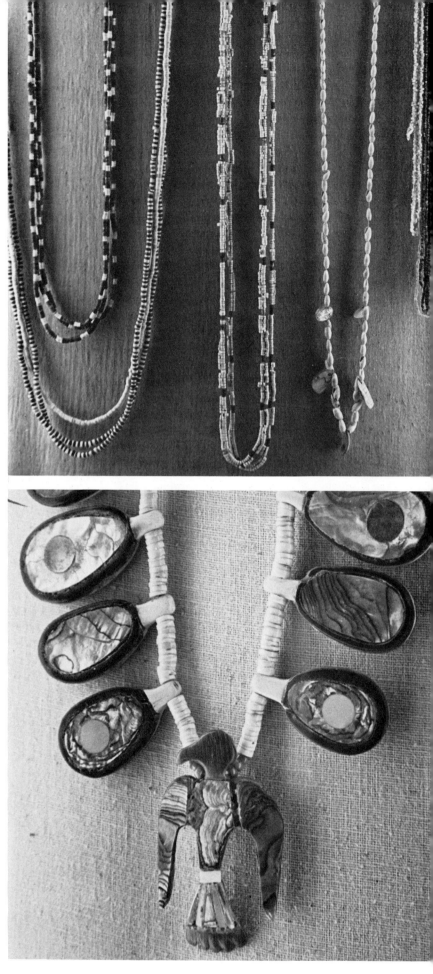

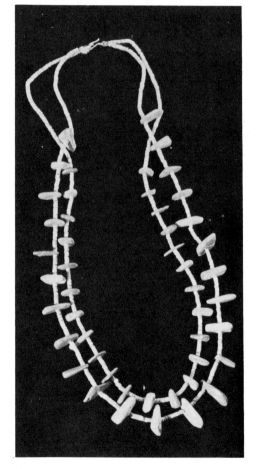

A typical American Indian necklace is made of turquoise with wampum shells between.
Collection, Mr. & Mrs. Wayne Chapman, Solana Beach, CA

Turquoise is one of many stones from which the bird symbol is carved. It appears in infinite combinations in American Indian jewelry.
Private collection

Above, left:
A beautifully beaded leather garment is worn with a string of beads and animal teeth around the neck. A strand of round glass beads is suspended from the bottom of the bodice. American Indian.
Collection, Field Museum of Natural History, Chicago

Above, right:
Multiple strands of shell beads may be worn with a costume that has glass beads sewn directly to the animal-skin clothing. Beading was frequently used to camouflage seams that could not be closed neatly because of the shape of the skins. Some glass beads are sewn to the headdress.
Collection, Field Museum of Natural History, Chicago

The American Indian male costume consists of shells, turquoise, beads around the neck and a belt of tiny feathers. Body painting is used for additional embellishment in many American Indian tribes and among African cultures as well.
Collection, Field Museum of Natural History, Chicago

A string of blue striped Venetian glass beads found in western African coastal countries. The loose beads are yellow, blue and red millefiore.
Collection, Dona Meilach

Beaded capes worn by the American Indians utilize small glass trade beads in different colors.
Collection, Field Museum of Natural History, Chicago

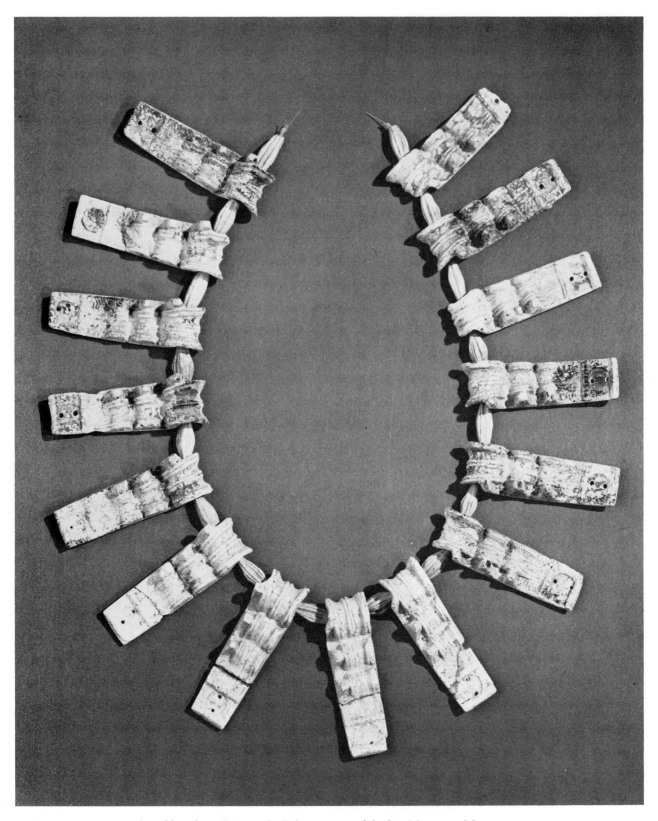

A necklace from Crete or the Peloponnesus of the late Minoan or Mycenaean period, 1400–1250 B.C., is made of translucent deep blue and aquamarine glass with thick white and light brown weathering crust on the surface. Probably made in a mold and the holes made while casting.
Collection and courtesy, The Corning Museum of Glass, Corning, NY

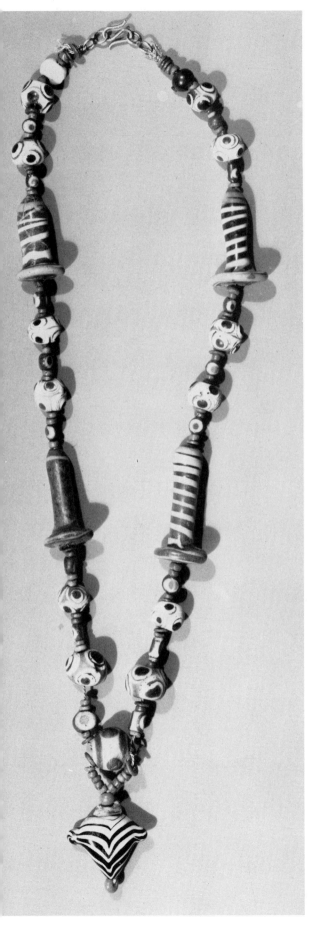

Opposite:
Ancient beads from Iran, second century B.C. to second century A.D., of bluish-green faience, white faience, carnelian and glazed steatite elements. "Faience" is a decorative glazed earthenware material similar to ceramic as we know it today.
Courtesy, The Corning Museum of Glass, Corning, NY

Left:
A necklace from Egypt, late eighteenth dynasty, 1400–1350 B.C. Translucent deep blue and opaque white glass. The large beads are shaped as "ear plugs" with an amulet at the bottom.
Courtesy, The Corning Museum of Glass, Corning, NY

Through the centuries and in every culture, bead shapes remain essentially the same. Contemporary painted ceramic beads by the people of Cuzco, Peru, are shaped and arranged much like the ancient beads from Egypt.
Collection, Dona Meilach

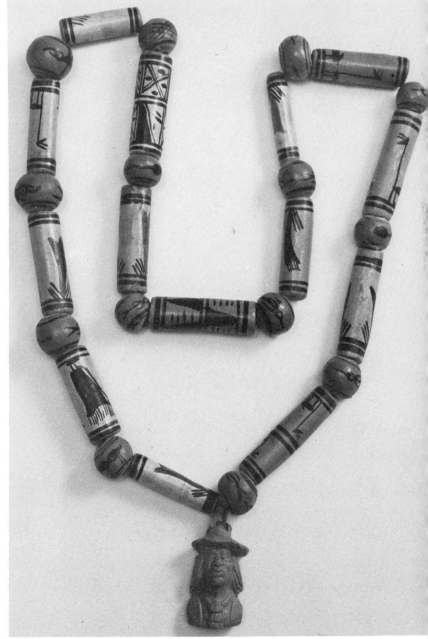

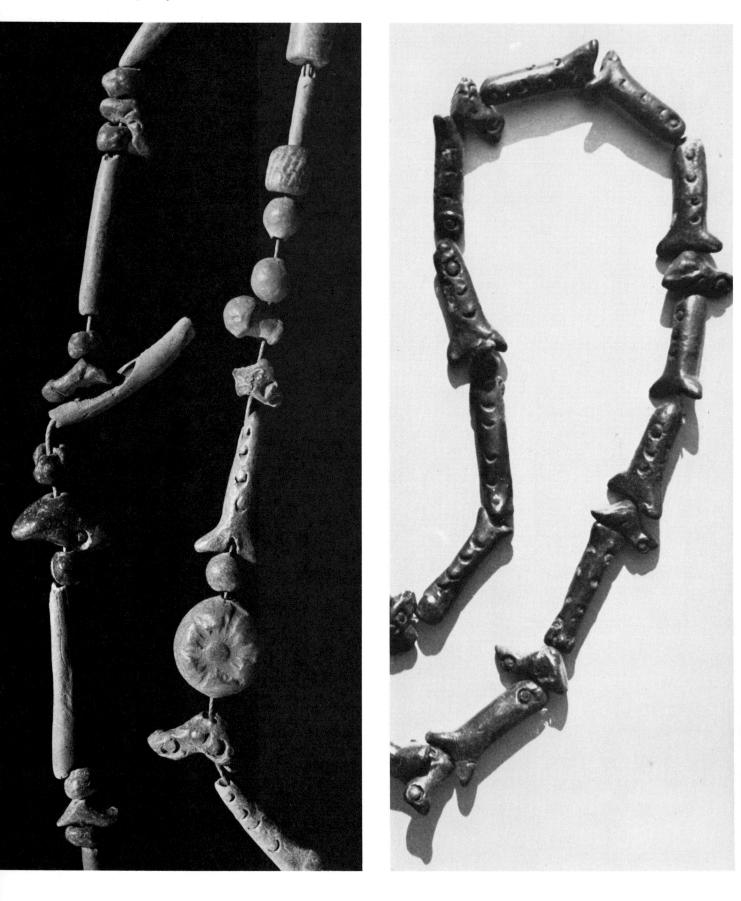

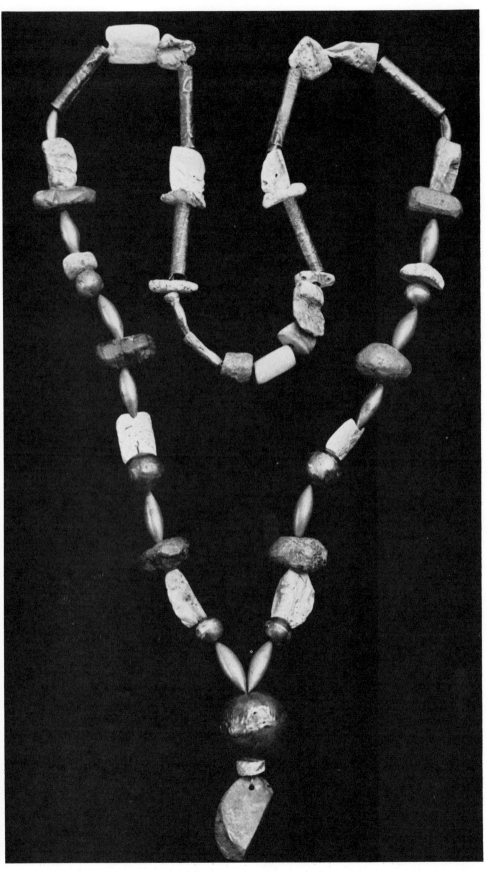

Opposite:
Clay beads in the shapes of fish and birds with some tubular shapes, rounds, and stylized flower pieces, are made in Mexico and strung in a variety of progressions. They are usually brightly colored, though some are used in the natural clay colors. Fish and birds are symbolic of fertility and good luck.
Photographed at the Casa de Pancho, San Diego, CA

Metal, turquoise, stone and pre-Colombian clay beads are combined in a necklace from Peru.
Collection, Dona Meilach

Necklaces purchased in Israel are composed of a variety of beads from different sources. Some are Phoenician glass from about 300 B.C. Others are glass "eye" beads probably of Venetian origin.
Collection, Helen Banes, Silver Spring, MD

Opposite, left:
A contemporary necklace made with glass beads from many sources. The large bead is a Venetian mostly orange millefiore (thousand flowers); the coral fluted beads and long glass beads are from Afghanistan. By Lee Erlin Snow, Los Angeles, CA.

Opposite, right:
A triple-strand necklace made by a contemporary designer has red and white heart beads from Guatemala interspersed with silver beads from Afghanistan and India. Some Venetian millefiore flat beads and flat coinlike tin shapes are also used. By Lee Erlin Snow, Los Angeles, CA.

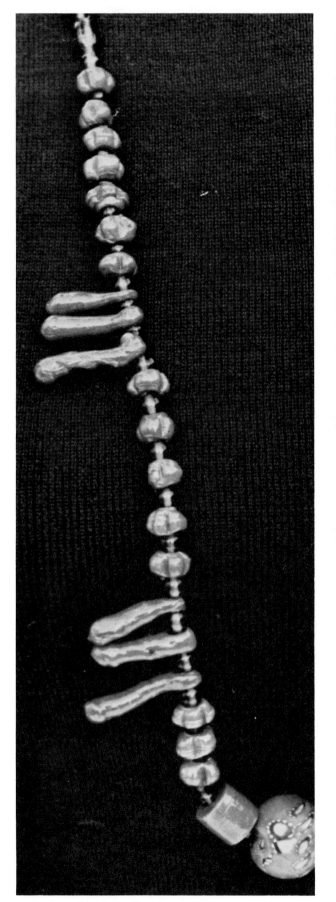

Above, left:
Colorful blue and yellow glass "eye" beads, with a tassel, were photographed in Guatemala, but the origin is probably Italian.

Above, right:
Multiple strands of striped glass beads are usually worn by the women of Ecuador around the neck, with plain beads on the wrists.

Right:
Glass beads with shaped large wood beads. Mexico.

Opposite:
Strands of glass beads hanging in the doorway of a souk (native market) in Tunisia are the same beads found in necklaces from many cultures. A majority of the glass beads are made in Venice and exported to different countries where they may be combined with seeds, pods, silver and other materials from a native area. It is difficult to identify the origin of a bead because of the vast amount of international trade that took place.

131

Beaded bands in a variety of arrangements are worn by the African people from different villages for armbands and ankle bands. Some are used as panels hanging from the belt. Beads are sewn to a cloth or skin backing.
Private collection

Blue-and-white beaded cloth mask and headdress from the Bamileke, the Cameroons, Africa. This is a secret society mask that is worn over a blue-and-white cotton robe.
Collection, Field Museum of Natural History, Chicago

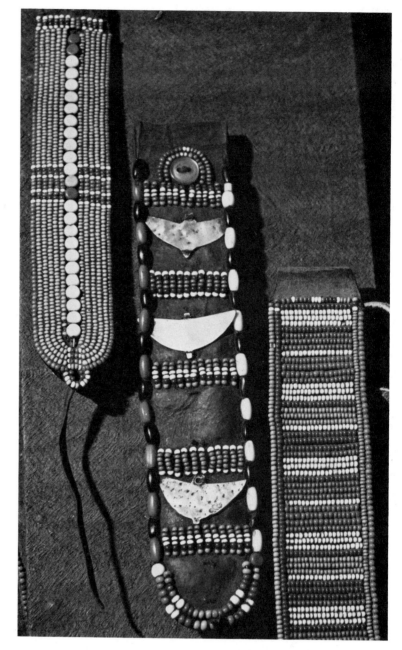

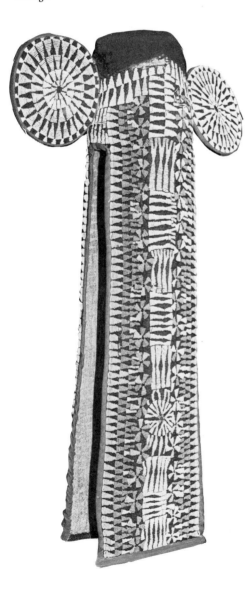

All beads are not strung on strands. For decorative garments, beads are often made into a fabric by weaving them on a loom (as do the American Indians), then couching, or stitching, the beaded fabric to the backing cloth. Another method is to sew a bead directly to the cloth individually with the needle and thread coming up and down. Or beads may be sewn on in multiples; that is, thread is brought up through the fabric, then laced through two, three or more beads before the thread is taken back down through the fabric.

The Masai large beaded collars *(at right)* are strung on wires, then each strand is wired to the previous strand so that the collars are stiff and can stand away from the body. For sewing beads to a garment, rolled palm fiber is used as the string medium. Beads are usually worn with a cotton toga. Ankle bracelets, wrist and arm bracelets are also part of the daily costume.

Beaded collars and earrings worn by the Masai women of southern Kenya are colorful and spectacular. The women shave their heads, and the collars are a bright contrast to their dark skins and the sameness of the desert in which they live. A large dance collar can weigh as much as eight pounds. Smaller collars are worn every day and in multiple layers.
Photo, courtesy, Lawrence Fine, San Diego, CA

The motif on the traditional "Kuchi," a dance dress from Afghanistan, is similar to the beaded roundel on the Mexican costume. It also illustrates a circle of beads sewn to a backing. Buttons and coins are added (detail).

The roundel is used in multiples and repeated in different sizes on the Afghanistan dress. Coins and amulets hang from the small rounds at the bottom. Additional jewelry, necklaces, earrings and bracelets are usually worn with the costume.
Private collection

Opposite:
A beaded circle on a costume from Mexico. Shells, sliced bone and horn and feathers are among the natural materials added to the headpiece.
Courtesy, Mexican National Tourist Council
Photo, The Lewis Co., Ltd.

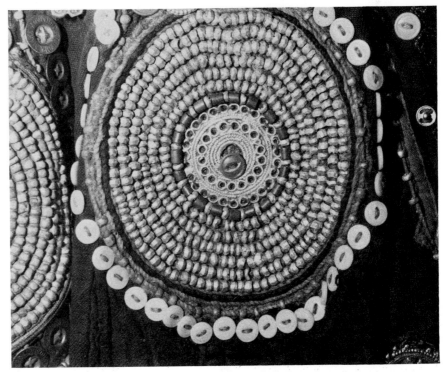

A large bead is composed of many small beads made in lanyard fashion with twin multiple strands of beads in a necklace from Morocco. Colors are bright, almost garish: red, black and yellow.

Techniques of beading and sewing are similar throughout the individual tribes; usage may be distinctive. An ornamental cape, belts and skirt are shown on the mannequin. They represent different styles of work in the Zulu costume of southeastern Africa.
Collection, Field Museum of Natural History, Chicago

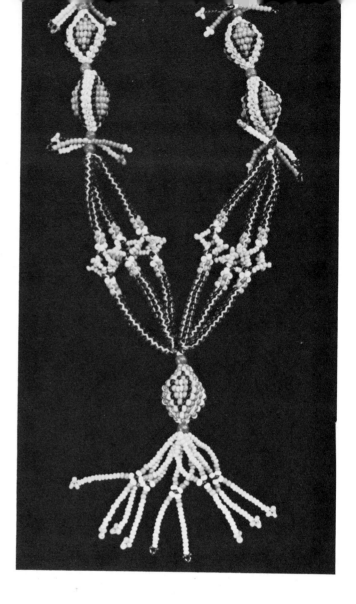

Detail of the design on a beaded loom-woven belt. American Indian.

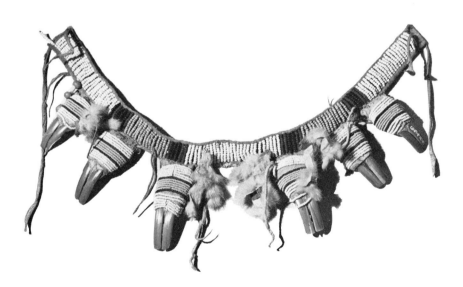

Top, left:
A neckpiece made in the shape of a rectangle with wrapped horsetail suspended in pendant fashion is sewn to the front of an American Indian garment.
Collection, Field Museum of Natural History, Chicago

Top, right:
Beads are spaced and sewn through the garment of an American Indian squaw's dress.
Collection, Field Museum of Natural History, Chicago

A necklace from the Crow tribe, American Indian, with lengths of sewn beads wrapped around an animal paw or claw.
Collection, Field Museum of Natural History, Chicago

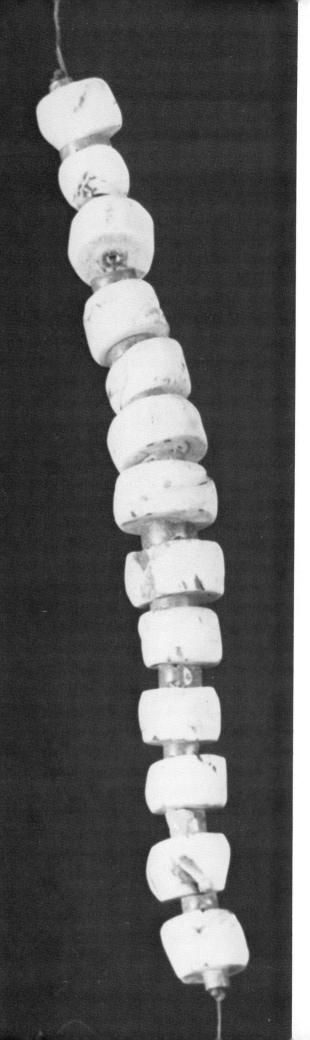

SHELLS, SEEDS, TEETH AND OTHER NATURAL OBJECTS

Seashells with holes created by the wear of the water were possibly the first forms to be used for body adornment by prehistoric man. In time he made holes in seeds, pods, teeth, bones and other objects in his environment. But beauty was not the only reason for adorning himself with strings of things. His life was fraught with fears, and the objects were believed to have a magical power to ward off evil and protect him from the menaces that threatened his life. The symbolic significance of many of the objects has been handed down through the ages.

Beads and amulets carved from bone expressed strength and power. The holes were made with other sharp natural materials; Eskimos today still use bone sharpened to a point as a drill, as did their ancestors thousands of years ago. African hunters hung animal teeth, bones and claws around their necks and waists as signs of their prowess and victories. Vertebral columns in the backs of animals, reptiles and fish have natural holes from the spinal cord. Lightweight vertebra bones have been part of tribal adornment in many countries since early times. In Kenya, a maiden's skirt hung with the vertebrae of fish symbolizes fertility.

In all cultures where it exists or is considered precious, the cowrie shell dominates. In Africa, the shells—originally collected from islands off the coast of East Africa—were valued as a medium of exchange just as were gold and beads. Cowrie shells, with their subtle female form, also symbolize fertility. When cowries are used to decorate ceremonial robes, headdresses, furniture and masks, they are considered a symbol of power and prestige.

Shells dominate in so many of the decorative arts of all the island cultures that it is hard to condense their story to a few pages. It is hoped that the following ideas will cause the reader to realize and to explore more deeply the use of shell as decoration in museum displays and in books. There are the tiniest sliced clam and oyster shells used in the Hishi necklaces from Hawaii. The same type of thin sliced beads is made from brown large shells by the people of India and Africa. Abalone shell is used for hundreds of purposes by the peoples throughout the Caribbean.

Combined with shells one frequently finds bones, teeth and other natural objects that are as varied in design and size as they are in usage by the people who select them and consider them valuable and important.

Slices of a very dense, solid seashell in graduated sizes are strung for a choker. The piece was purchased from an Afghanistan trader, but probably is not of Afghani origin because such shells are not indigenous to the area.
Collection, Mr. & Mrs. Wayne Chapman, Solana Beach, CA

Cowrie shells are strung and suspended from a Tibetan belt buckle. The belt typically is worn at the center waist and the cowrie strands hang over the abdomen and crotch. *Collection, Mr. & Mrs. Wayne Chapman, Solana Beach, CA*

Right: Detail.

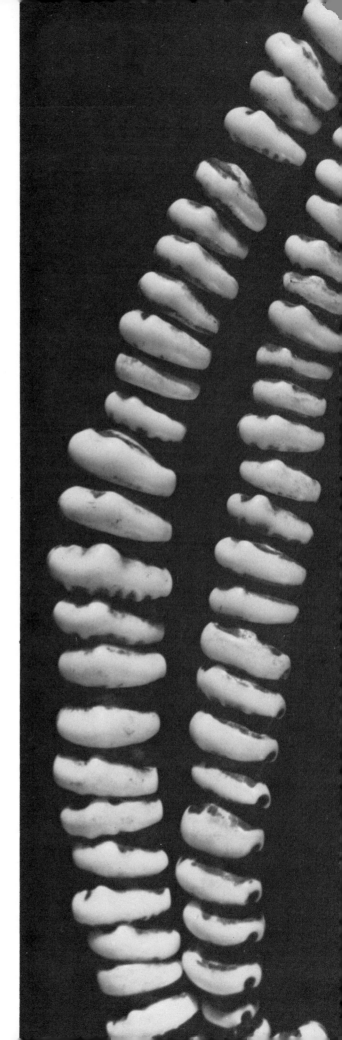

140

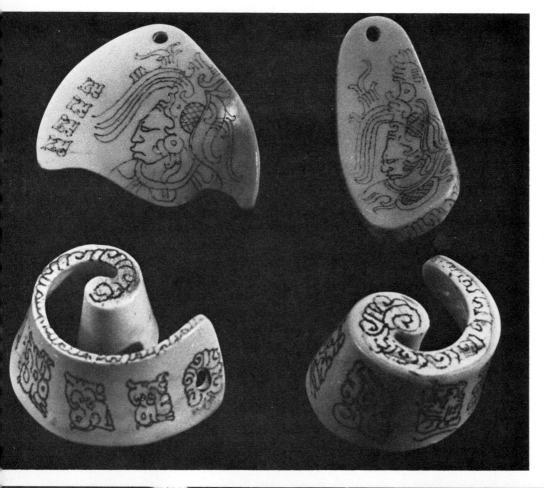

Sliced portions of shells are smoothed, then engraved with designs by people of Mexico. The designs are of dancers, warriors or some symbology of the particular area in which they are made. After the designs are engraved in the white shell, dark ink is rubbed in to make the line stand out. *Courtesy, The Casa de Pancho, San Diego, CA*

Hishi style (flat disc) oyster-shell beads from the Philippines are extremely tiny (the top two examples). *Bottom:* A Hawaiian Niihau shell lei with a snail shell. *Collection, Dona Meilach*

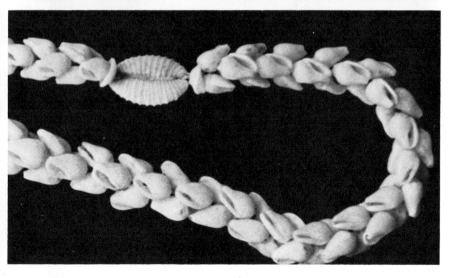

A variety of shell leis from Hawaii. Shells are gathered and sorted, then strung in single, double or triple layers. The arrangement may represent a flower. These museum examples were used for barter. The selection of shells from Hawaii is incredible.

A New Guinea procession shows the array of large kina shells hanging on the chests of the men. Bones, cowrie and other shells are used in nose rings, necklaces, headdress and leg pieces.
Courtesy, Field Museum of Natural History, Chicago

Above, right:
Kina shell necklace, New Guinea. These large iridescent shells are used as money or as a sign of wealth. They may be worn as earrings, armbands or as a panel down the front of a person's clothes. It is not uncommon to see as many as twenty or thirty strung from the neck to the hem of a garment.
Collection, Steve and Susan Nelson, Palos Verdes Estates, CA

A hunter of the Kau people, Africa, wears cowrie shells, armbands and shell jewelry, Often the face and body are thoroughly painted in a marvelous arrangement of abstract designs.

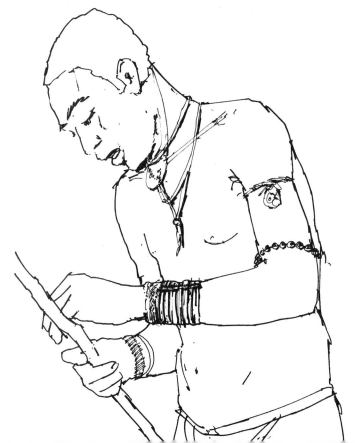

142

A shell bracelet from the Philippines. The long white bead in the front is a hair bead, probably made from a bird bone.
Collection, Mr. & Mrs. Wayne Chapman, Solana Beach, CA

The men of the Masai, Africa, wear cowrie-shell body jewelry and feathered headdresses. Their face painting appears as shell forms, too.
Photo, courtesy, Lawrence Fine, San Diego, CA

Sliced and carved shells. Africa.

Lower right:
Carved shell with beads. American Indian.

Opposite:
Bones, teeth, beads, small animal and reptile skulls, silver and glass beads, dominate the costume of a Mexican dancer.
Courtesy, Mexican National Tourist Council

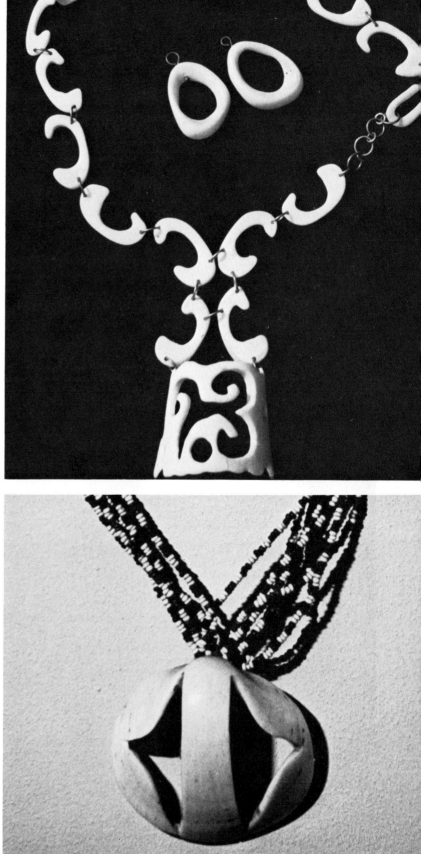

Sliced shells and bones with shell and glass are used in the decorations worn by the Samburu warriors of Kenya, Africa.

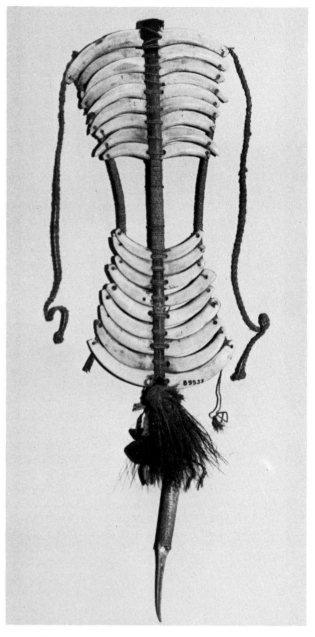

Breast ornament made of bone and dried sea-weed. Lottin Islands, Melanesia.
Collection, Field Museum of Natural History, Chicago

Breast ornament of bones and wood with fiber-wrapped portions. Melanesia.
Collection, Field Museum of Natural History, Chicago

Opposite:
Breast ornament of feathers and shells. Marquesas, Polynesia.
Courtesy, Field Museum of Natural History, Chicago

Neck ornament of tusks and braided plant fibers. The Igorot of North Luzon, Philippine Islands.
Collection, Field Museum of Natural History, Chicago

Lower right:
Animal claws with fur are strung, as beads, for the chest ornament of an American Indian warrior.
Collection, Field Museum of Natural History, Chicago

Below:
Jewelry design and its use are often shown in tribal ritual and symbolic items. The Kachina doll mirrors the real life use of body decoration—how the masks are painted and how moccasins are designed by the Hopi Indians of Arizona.
Collection, San Diego Museum of Man, California

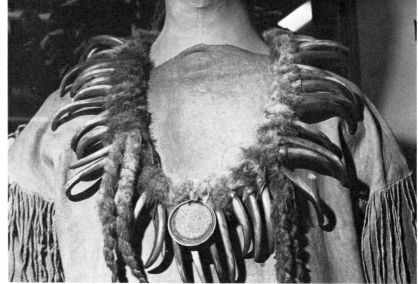

A shell necklace from the Philippine Islands.
Private collection

A large shell pendant with Indian wampum and glass beads. American Indian.
Collection, Field Museum of Natural History, Chicago

Leather and fur necklace with a piece of bone. Africa.
Collection, Mrs. Robert Rothschild, Northbrook, IL

Carrying pouch of leather with woven brown and white leather strips and braided cord. The cover lifts with a sinew "lock" that pulls through a hole to keep it secured. Africa.
Collection, Dona Meilach

Choker of leather, white bone and dark stone beads. Africa.
Collection, Mrs. Robert Rothschild, Northbrook, IL

An African wedding doll from the Turkana tribe (front and back views). Materials are leather, wood beads, shells and an old zipper down both sides of the figure.
Collection, Steve and Susan Nelson, Palos Verdes Estates, CA

Another version of the African wedding doll from the Lake Rudolph area. The base of the doll is wood. Similar dolls are made by the Zulus; but the basis is often fabric rather than wood, and they are used to identify tribes because each tribe uses its own arrangements of beads.
Collection, Mr. & Mrs. Wayne Chapman, Solana Beach, CA

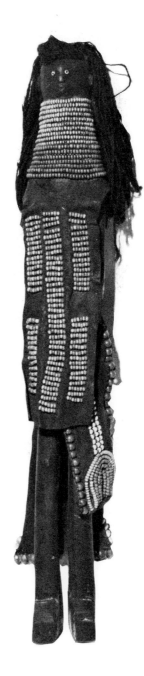

Cowrie shells edge the neckline and sleeves of an African tribal shirt that is laden with rectangular fetish mirrors. The mirrors are believed to ward off evil spirits.
Collection, Roger Brown, Chicago, IL

Opposite:
Boar's tusks are combined with hammered silver. The pendant represents the Rama-yana Demon and has a tongue and eyes of mother-of-pearl. Bali.

A single boar's tooth is fitted into a silver cap and suspended from a braided silver chain. Thailand.
Collection, Steve and Susan Nelson, Palos Verdes Estates, CA

Shell necklace with cloth dolls of the Seri Indians, of Seriland, northern Mexico.
Collection, Mrs. Robert Rothschild, North-brook, IL

Assorted necklaces from South America illustrate the use of seeds and hard fruits:

Left:
Natural colors of seeds that vary from white to black and red are used in a necklace from Venezuela.

Center:
Black seeds are strung in groups of three with smaller seed beads between. A large pod becomes the central pendant with dangling bead strands beneath. Venezuela.

Right:
Painted seeds with natural color seeds are combined with porcupine quills and feathers wrapped in. Brazil.
Collection, Helen Banes, Silver Springs, MD

Seed bead necklace with acorns and other hard-fruit nuts.

In South America, Central America, Africa, New Guinea and wherever there is lush forestation, many of the plants yield hard seeds, fruits and pods that dry and last indefinitely. Such plant parts are often drilled through and used for a variety of beads with incredible shapes, colors and textures. They are strung together in an infinite range of jewelry pieces and worn for daily and ceremonial occasions.

Seeds and dhoum palm nuts are popular for beads in neckwear of East Africa. The large kernels are collected by the tribesmen and carved with circles, feathers or leaf-shaped designs. When portions of the dark surface are carved away, the contrast of pattern results. Necklaces of these nuts are also worn around the necks of young camels to ward off illness. The white discs are made from ostrich eggshells that have been sliced.

Below:
The outer necklace is made of plant stems cut into small pieces and lacquered so they appear as natural wood. Thailand.

The inner necklace is made of the round tiny Hawaiian seashells combined with flat seeds. The shells are gray with brown striations so they coordinate with the brown seeds.
Collection, Dona Meilach

Large and small tree fruits and smaller plant seeds and nuts are used in this necklace from Cuzco, Peru. The nut in the center is carved in the shape of a face.
Collection, Dona Meilach

Lacquer and tortoiseshell hair ornaments from Japan in the forms of combs, "kushi"; tapered sticks, "kogai"; and two-pronged needles, "kanzashi," of the seventeenth and eighteenth centuries are now collectors' items. One end of the kogai is removable so the stick can be put through the hair.

Collection, Mr. & Mrs. Wayne Chapman, Solana Beach, CA

In Japan, hair jewels in the forms of combs called *kushi*, sticks called *kogai* and two-pronged hair needles called *kanzashi* flourished for use with the elegant hairstyles worn by Japanese women. At one point in history, many beaded and dangling imagery pieces were added to hair ornaments. Often the symbolic designs acted as talismans for the wearer. There were miniature water wheels, windmills, ships and butterflies that shimmered and dangled as the wearer moved. At one time strict edicts were issued for less frivolous pursuits, so the public pressed makers of *kanzashi* to create tiny spoonlike ends to the ornaments that they might be considered to be ear-cleaning instruments; then they could pass the imposed regulations and be classified as useful items rather than pure adornment.

Designs on Japanese hair ornaments included flowers, whole scenes from daily life, mythical figures, gardens and poems. They were often made of wood lacquerwork, tortoiseshell or ivory. The extensive use of hair ornaments can be observed in Japanese scrolls and prints of the seventeenth to nineteenth centuries.

Hair combs of different materials—whalebone, straw, shell and wood—have been made and used by many societies. So ornate and decorative are they that they have provided inspiration for contemporary artists as objects of sculptural form (see page 72).

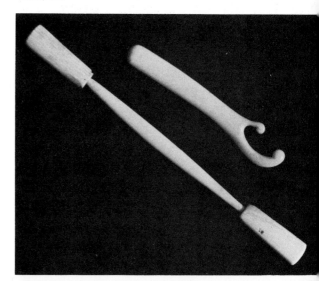

Assorted hair pieces show the imagination in design and the use of indigenous materials of a given society.

Left:
Wood, probably Indonesian.

Below:
Silver. Chinese.

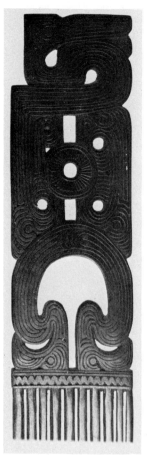

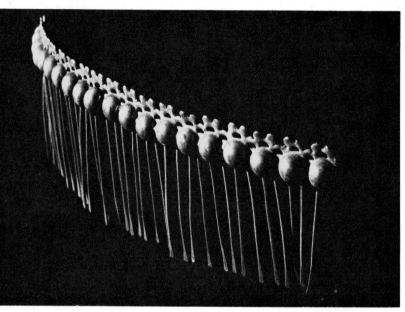

Above:
Wood with beads. Philippines.

Right:
Straw. New Guinea.
Collection, Mr. & Mrs. Wayne Chapman, Solana Beach, CA

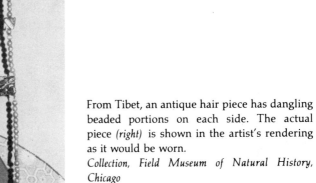

From Tibet, an antique hair piece has dangling beaded portions on each side. The actual piece *(right)* is shown in the artist's rendering as it would be worn.
Collection, Field Museum of Natural History, Chicago

A Japanese doll represents the formally costumed Japanese woman. Just as armor and weapons were regarded as artful objects for the men, hair ornaments, kimono and obi were the art forms for the women of old Japan. Because the patterned kimono and obi of the geishas and courtesans were so opulent in fabric and design, jewelry such as necklaces and earrings worn by the Europeans was out of place and superfluous. Hence, the hair ornaments.

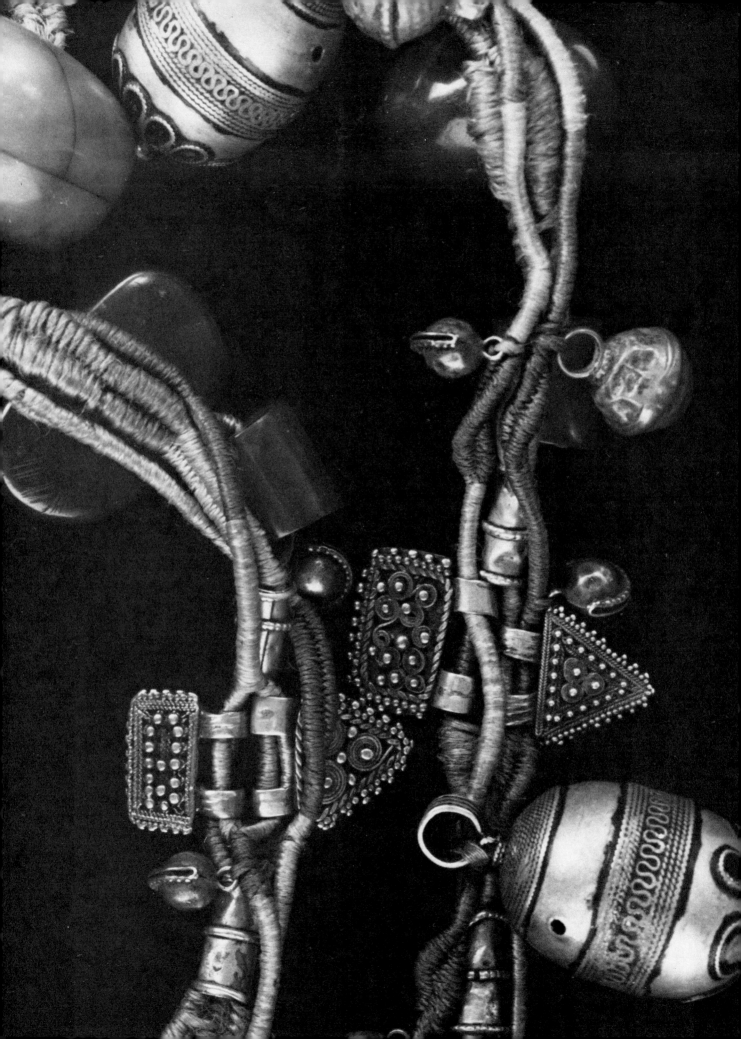

7 Putting It All Together

Ethnic jewelry by contemporary craftspeople results in a unique type of expressiveness. Combining beads from one or more cultures gives those who appreciate the beads an opportunity to fashion them in a new way and to adapt them to Western styles. When each strand of beads, each bracelet or other adornment is worn with a contemporary garment, all take on a new life, a new vibrancy.

Contemporary craftspeople do not wish to imitate or display jewelry in the same manner as the Berber woman or the Japanese courtesan. The beads, far removed from their origin and costume, are usually worn with more restraint than the originals. The object is to create something new and unusual with something odd and beautiful. Every object need not be of ethnic origin; anything may be combined so long as good taste and artistic unity are present.

Is the approach successful? The following examples will let you be the judge. They are only a few samples of the countless combinations that may be created using the beads as the medium and ethnic design as inspiration. Perhaps they will whet your appetite to create your own jewelry.

How can you begin?

Primarily, you must have the beads or know where to get them. Sources are not hard to find, but locating them may take a new awareness and some legwork. Look for commercial bead sources in the craft magazines and bead publications listed in the Bibliography. Names and addresses of current suppliers are not included; such lists become outdated quickly. Sources move, change names, go out of business. There may be sources in your city that do not advertise, so the list would be incomplete.

Begin to look for the kinds of pieces you see throughout the book, and collect them until you have a private cache from which you can begin to arrange and rearrange beads into fashion delights that will never go out of date. They will always elicit a response when you wear them because they will be so completely different from the mass-produced jewelry one can buy.

The best and cheapest source for ethnic beads is to buy them when you visit any of the countries. What if you can't travel? Then

Opposite:
Details of the necklace on page 163 illustrate the ideas and materials used when a contemporary artist combines beads from ethnic cultures with varied craft techniques. Barbara Chapman used wrapped yarns for a multiple-strand necklace with amber, agate, Ethiopian fetishes, beads and bells and other objects.

Many African tribeswomen string beads on their hair in long and short arrangements. An adaptation of the tribal hairdo became popular in the 1980s as a result of a movie that featured beaded hair as "novel."

Wrapped fibers are brought through an Oriental jade pi with glass beads, silver beads and coins added. By Nancy Inman.

Opposite:
A leather flint pouch from Tibet set with sliver domes and a polished stone was used to carry flint. The pouches predate matches. Such pouches were used in Afghanistan, China, Burma. The striker is along the bottom of the pouch. It is used as a pendant with Ethiopian silver and amber beads and designed to be worn as a necklace or belt. By Barbara Chapman.

Japanese coins have ready-made holes perfect for stringing onto a necklace with glass beads from Taiwan and silver beads from India. Detail. By Dona Meilach.

use other people's travel to your advantage. Seek out garage sales in wealthy communities. One person's castoff may be another's treasure. Flea markets are based on that premise. They offer a wealth of bead sources.

Some of the best finds are in secondhand stores or resale outlets. A necklace brought home from a trip to Hawaii, or to the Caribbean, by one person may have lost its zest and novelty for the owner. The jewelry designer may envision those beads as the beginning of a stunning necklace.

For unusual shells with holes already drilled, purchase ready-made necklaces from other countries that you will find in museum shops, in tourist shops, at zoos and other places. The necklaces are inexpensive and can be cut apart and the shells used in new arrangements. If you collect shells, you can drill holes in them with hand or power tools and fine drill bits.

Above:
A necklace of snake vertebrae, amber, ivory and jade. By Barbara Chapman. See detail, page 112.

Above, right:
A pin weaving creates a fiber backing for a collection of Nepalise, African and Chinese beads that are hung on a Chinese decoration taken from another context. The strung beads are Chinese fetishes, African trading beads, jade and bone. By Barbara Chapman.

Right:
Abstract whale necklace with cloisonné beads. There are antique Roman glass iridescent dark blue beads, amber, trade beads and many other precious items in the strand. See detail, page 101. By Barbara Chapman.

A strip of leather has been beaded with fine seed beads, then stuffed and made into a tubular "strand." Glass beads, ceramic beads, liquid silver beads and beach stones polished by nature have been added to create a bib necklace based on American Indian concepts. By Lucia.
Collection, Dona Meilach

Silver beads and metal coins must be ferreted out wherever you can locate them. Many countries circulate coins that already have holes in them. I treasured, and eventually used in a necklace, Japanese coins with holes in the center that I brought home several years ago.

As an intrepid bead seeker, you will learn to check the classified and display ads in local publications and in the yellow pages of telephone books in your own city and in any city you may visit. Look under "jewelry," "crafts," "beads," "boutiques," "imports." You may find individual beads and unusual strands of jewelry in galleries and shops that sell ethnic clothing and crafts. Once your bead antennae are up, you will be amazed at what you can discover.

To string beads with tiny holes, use rattail cord, waxed linen, nylon, plastic-coated wire or dental floss. Thin wire stringing needles are available. For beads with large holes, use thicker string material such as braided rayon, shoelaces and wrapped fibers. Adhere beads to woven and crocheted collars. Stitch short lengths of

"You've Gotta Have Heart, Find the Key to My Heart!" is the title of Helen Banes's necklace. Each necklace is a statement as a work of art. The tapestry-woven collar in turquoise, gray, coral, garnet and beige combines fibers from many countries. On the collar are sewn or threaded silver elements: a heart from Islam, leaf pendants from Iran, keys from India, beads from Ethiopia, an ebony bead with a silver inlay from India, a silver disc from Afghanistan and a barrel-shaped bead from Ethiopia. Venetian glass beads are combined with bauxite from West Africa and ceramic beads from the United States. Semiprecious stones are the amethyst from India and the garnet from Iran.

beads to garments wherever you will feel comfortable with the way they look. If you have only one dynamic bead, string it on braided silk and add a tassel in Oriental style. Take your cue from the various cultures and tuck beads into a hairdo, wear a length from a fibula pinned to a garment, hang beads from a belt, cuff or armband. Observe, too, how beads are made and used in multiple strands.

Dare to be different, original, with the jewelry you create and wear. Ethnic goes everywhere, every day, at every age.

The Berber bib combines silver embroidery thread, France; copper-colored thread, Italy; blue silk with nylon, Brazil; perle cotton, Switzerland; wool, Denmark and England. The silver pendant and coins are from Afghanistan, Ethiopia and India; the glass beads are from Italy; coral and enamel beads are from Morocco. By Helen Banes.

The pectoral piece titled "Homage to Tutankhamen" uses variegated colored threads woven across into the central portion of a large silver pendant from Afghanistan. The weaving is a unique addition to and adaptation of an object. By Helen Banes.

A handle from an African copper pot becomes a purse handle. A beaded roundel from an Afghanistan dress, Afghani tassels and silver beads all combine in a woven fabric purse. By Barbara Chapman.

Left:
The metal portion of a torque neckpiece has been used upside down as the handle for a purse with Afghanistan silver and Chinese embroidery added. By Barbara Chapman.

A woven beaded necklace combines an American Indian technique with a pre-Hispanic design. By Linda Jones.

Right:
Tassels, emulating those used on fabrics from India and Afghanistan, are beaded with assorted glass beads. By Kathy Malec.

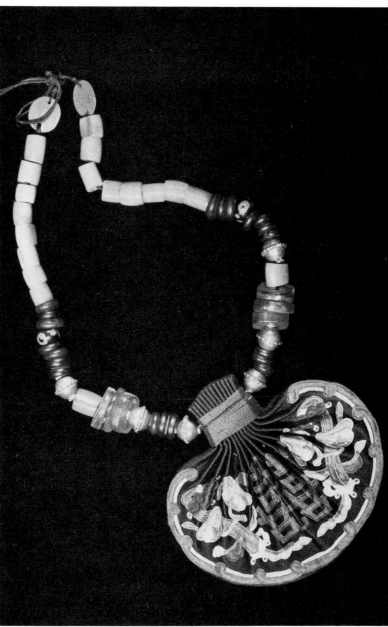

A Chinese pleated sachet trimmed with gold braid is strung as the pendant for a necklace using silver, carnelian, glass beads and coins. *Private collection*

Left:
Wrapped and knotted necklace of fibers with glass beads. By Kathy Malec.

A cast bronze pendant of the Kirdi, an African tribe, represents a banana leaf, which symbolizes a woman's transition from childhood to adulthood. It is strung with Kirdi bronze bells and shells from Africa and combined with glass "eye" and other beads from Italy. By Harriet Arenson.
Collection, Dona Meilach

The necklace ending illustrated is made of wrapped fibers; some of the wrappings appear as hishi beads, by the use of alternating color wraps. The cowrie shells emulate the use of the shell by many cultures. By combining feathers and rough, hairy yarns an ethnic appearance results. Similar endings may be found on wall hangings and belts by today's fiber artists.

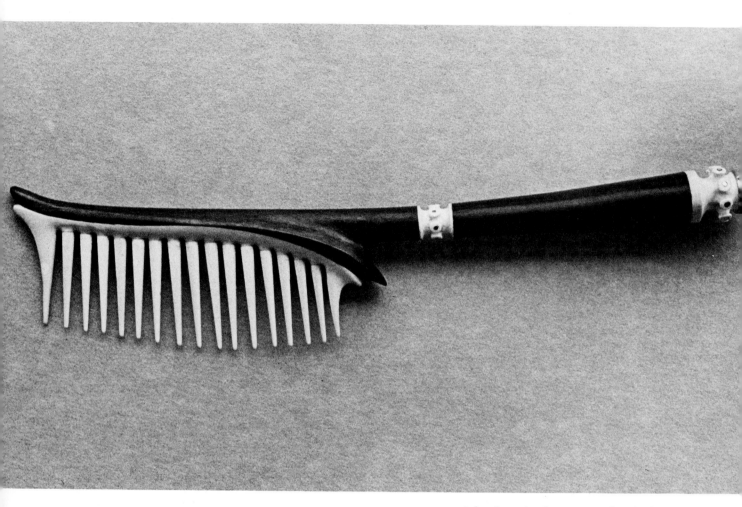

A hand comb of ivory, wood and silver. By Frank E. Cummings III.

Opposite:
Contemporary necklace by Betty Hertzmark is composed of ceramic fish, birds and beads from Mexico and French brass beads.

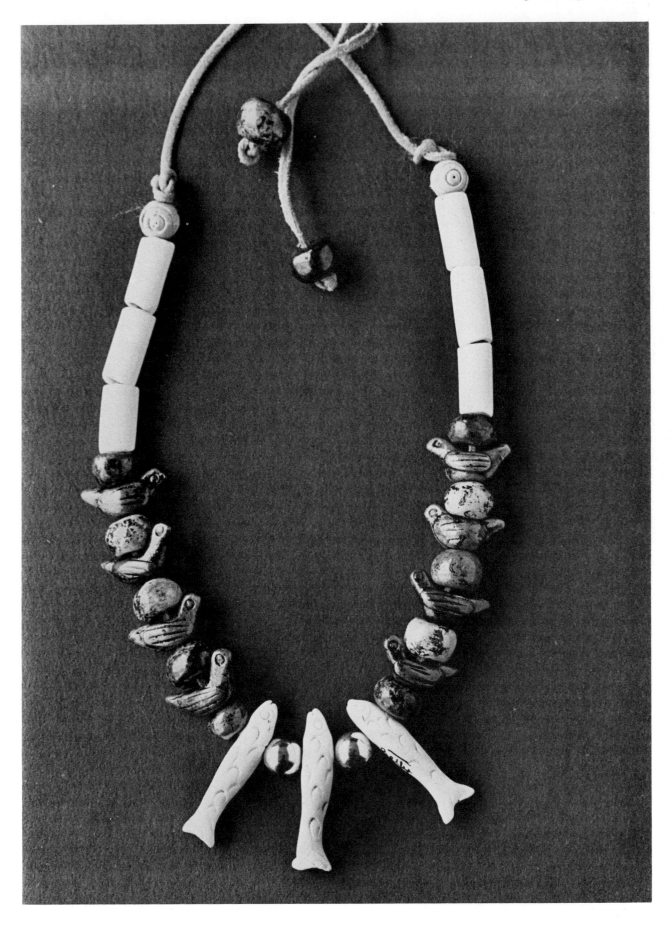

Hand-carved ivory pendants with feathers inspired by crafts from Ghana. By Frank E. Cummings III.

Opposite:
Kitty necklace; a charm necklace with the peach stone Chinese symbols in silver, carved ojimi beads and vertebra bones with assorted glass and stone beads. By Barbara Chapman.

Selected Bibliography

The history of jewelry is almost as old as man himself. Certainly it dates back to the beginning of art history. Many publications thoroughly cover the very ornate jeweled pieces worn by royalty and aristocracy and that have been in museum collections throughout the world. There have been many studies made about isolated tribes, ancient techniques, individual types of beads and so forth. Such articles appear in scholarly publications throughout the world and may be written in English, Dutch, German, French and so forth. I have researched much of this material, but frequently the articles are difficult to find, esoteric and disappointing. Often days of searching out one article with a provocative title resulted in little or no more information than I already had. Yet I am sure that much has been and will be written that could add nuggets of exciting information.

Your own research into any aspect of jewelry might begin with the volumes listed. Also refer to the bibliography in each volume for other avenues of research.

I have chosen to list publications that are readily available in large public libraries or in college art libraries and those that shed most light on a subject.

At the time of this compilation, interest in ethnic jewelry is increasing. I have seen advertisements listed in *Publishers Weekly* for new books about the body adornments of individual groups. As publication date is in advance of actual publication, I cannot list these without seeing them. To keep up to date, refer to current research tools listed on page 179.

BERNES, J. P. *Costumes Broderies Brocarts MAROC.* Paris: C.P.I.P., 1974.

BERNES, J. P., AND ALAIN JACOB. *Armes, Bijoux, Ceramiques MAROC.* Paris: C.P.I.P., 1974.

BLACK, J. ANDERSON. *The Story of Jewelry.* New York: William Morrow and Company, Inc., 1974.

BOVIN, MURRAY. *Jewelry Making for Schools, Tradesmen, Craftsmen.* Forest Hills, New York: Bovin Publishing Company, 1967.

BOWIE, HAMISH. *Jewelry Making.* Chicago: Henry Regnery Company, 1976.

BUSHELL, RAYMOND. *The Wonderful World of Netsuke.* Vermont and Tokyo: Charles E. Tuttle Company, 1964.

DAVIS, MARY L., AND GRETA PACK. *Mexican Jewelry.* Austin, Texas: University of Texas Press, 1963.

DE GOLISH, VITOLD. *Primitive India* (Nadine Peppard, trans.). New York: E. P. Dutton and Company, Inc., 1954.

Deeson, A.F.L. (ed.). *The Collector's Encyclopedia of Rocks and Minerals.* New York: Clarkson N. Potter, Inc., 1973.

Enciso, Jorge. *Design Motifs of Ancient Mexico.* New York: Dover Publications, Inc., 1953.

Erikson, Jean Mowat. *The Universal Bead.* New York: W. W. Norton, 1969.

Ferguson, George. *Signs and Symbols in Christian Art.* New York: Oxford University Press, 1966.

Garside, Anne (ed.). *Jewelry Ancient to Modern.* The Walters Art Gallery, Baltimore. New York: The Viking Press, 1979.

Gerlach, Martin (ed.). *Primitive and Folk Jewelry.* New York: Dover Publications, Inc., 1971.

Goetz, Hermann. *The Art of India.* 2nd ed. New York: The Greystone Press, 1964.

Goldemberg, Rose Leiman, and Edward R. Height, Jr. *Antique Jewelry: A Practical and Passionate Guide.* New York: Crown Publishers, Inc., 1976.

Gordon, Albert F., and Leonard Kahan. *The Tribal Bead.* New York: The Tribal Arts Gallery, Inc., 1976.

Gregorietti, Guido. *Jewelry through the Ages.* New York: American Heritage, 1969.

Henderson, John W., et al. *Area Handbook for Oceania.* Foreign Area Studies of The American University, Washington, D.C. Washington, D.C.: Superintendent of Documents, U.S. Government Printing Office., 1971.

Huet, Michel. *The Dance, Art and Ritual of Africa.* New York: Pantheon Books, 1978.

Hughes, Graham. *The Art of Jewelry.* New York: The Viking Press, 1972.

Morton, Philip. *Contemporary Jewelry.* New York: Holt, Rinehart, and Winston, Inc., 1970.

Murphy, Marjorie. *Beadwork of American Indian Designs.* New York: Watson-Guptill Publications, 1974.

New International Illustrated Encyclopedia of Art, The. Vol. 1 (Aachen-Architectural Terms). New York: The Greystone Press, 1967.

————. Vol. 2 (Architectural Terms-Baroque Art and Architecture). New York: The Greystone Press, 1967.

————. Vol. 12 (Inman-Le Clerc Family). New York: The Greystone Press, 1967.

Newman, Thelma R. *Contemporary African Arts and Crafts.* New York: Crown Publishers, Inc., 1974.

————. *Contemporary Southeast Asian Arts and Crafts.* New York: Crown Publishers, Inc., 1977.

Nuttall, Zelia (ed.). *The Codex Nuttall.* New York: Dover Publications, Inc., 1975.

Orchard, William C. *Beads and Beadwork of the American Indians.* New York: Museum of the American Indian, Heye Foundation, 1929.

Pack, Greta. *Chains and Beads.* Princeton, New Jersey: D. Van Nostrand Company, Inc., 1951.

————. *Jewelry Making for the Beginning Craftsman.* Princeton, New Jersey: D. Van Nostrand Company, Inc., 1957.

Parker, Ann, and Avon Neal. *Molas: Folk Art of the Cuna Indians.* New York: Clarkson N. Potter, Inc., 1977.

Riefenstahl, Leni. *The People of Kau.* New York: Harper & Row, Publishers, 1976.

Runes, Dagobert D., and Harry G. Schrickel (eds.). *Encyclopedia of the Arts.* New York: Philosophical Library, 1946.

Ryerson, Egerton. *The Netsuke of Japan.* New York: Castle Books, 1958.

Shaffer, Frederick W. *Indian Designs from Ancient Ecuador.* New York: Dover Publications, Inc., 1979.

Stribling, Mary Lou. *Crafts from North American Indian Arts.* New York: Crown Publishers, Inc., 1975.

Toneyama, Kojin. *The Popular Arts of Mexico.* Tokyo and New York: Heibonsha, 1972; John Weatherhill, Inc., 1974.

TROWELL, MARGARET, AND HANS NEVERMANN. *African and Oceanic Art.* New York: Harry N. Abrams, Inc., 1968.

UNTRACHT, OPPI. *Metal Techniques for Craftsmen.* Garden City, New York: Doubleday & Co., Inc., 1975.

VON NEUMANN, ROBERT. *The Design and Creation of Jewelry.* rev. ed. Radnor, Pennsylvania: Chilton Book Company, 1972.

WAHLMAN, MAUDE. *Contemporary African Arts.* Chicago: Field Museum of Natural History, 1974.

WILSON, HENRY. *Silverwork & Jewellery.* London: Pitman Publ., Ltd., 1902 and 1978.

Articles

ALLEN, JAMEY D. "Amber and Its Substitutes." *The Bead Journal,* vol. 2, Spring 1976, pp. 11–12.

"Gold of El Dorado, The Heritage of Columbia." *Field Museum of Natural History Bulletin,* vol. 51, no. 4, April 1980.

KESHISHIAN, JOHN M., M.D. "Anatomy of a Burmese Beauty Secret." *National Geographic,* June 1979, pp. 798–801.

KIRTLEY, MICHAEL AND AUBINE. "The Inadan: Artisans of the Sahara." *National Geographic,* August 1979, pp. 282–298.

KOPROWSKI, PAUL. "Combs of the Beni-Amur." *African Arts,* vol. IX, no. 3, April 1976.

LAMB, ALASTAIR. "Krobo Powder-Glass Beads." *African Arts,* vol. IX, No. 3, April 1976.

ZIESNITZ, SHARON. "Of Combs, Hair-Needles and Butterflies." *Orientations,* vol. 10, no. 5, May 1979. (Hong Kong: Pacific Magazines, Ltd.)

The following publications regularly publish articles about jewelry:

GEMS AND MINERALS
Box 687
Mentone, CA 92359

GLASS ART MAGAZINE
Box 7529
Oakland, CA 94601

GOLDSMITHS' JOURNAL
Published by The Society of North
   American Goldsmiths
c/o Art Department
Longwood College
Farmville, VA 23901

LAPIDARY JOURNAL
3564 Kettner Boulevard
Box 80937
San Diego, CA 92138

ORNAMENT (formerly THE BEAD
   JOURNAL)
1221 South La Cienega
Box 35029
Los Angeles, CA 90035

Articles about ethnic cultures may be found in such publications as:

AFRICAN ARTS
University of California
African Studies Center
405 Hilgard Avenue
Los Angeles, CA 90024

AMERICAN ETHNOLOGIST
1703 New Hampshire Avenue
   N.W.
Washington, D.C. 20009

MANKIND
Mankind Publishing Company
8060 Melrose Avenue
Los Angeles, CA 90046

NATIONAL GEOGRAPHIC MAGAZINE
National Geographic Society
17th and M Streets N.W.
Washington, D.C. 20036

SMITHSONIAN
900 Jefferson Drive
Washington, D.C. 20560

Also look for articles in regional and national general-interest publications.

To locate articles/magazines/books about specific countries and cultures, consult the following research sources (available in most libraries):

ART INDEX R. R. Bowker Company 1180 Avenue of the Americas New York, NY 10036	Monthly listing of articles about art in selected art publications.
BOOKS IN PRINT R. R. Bowker Company 1180 Avenue of the Americas New York, NY 10036	Guide to published books, by subject and author. Also forthcoming books.
THE ENCYCLOPEDIA OF ASSOCIATIONS Gale Research Company Book Tower Detroit, MI 48226	Listing of associations by name and category, noting those that publish journals. Check headings: Anthropology, Archeology, Art, Crafts, Ethnology.
THE OFFICIAL MUSEUM DIRECTORY American Association of Museums 1055 Jefferson Street N.W. Washington, D.C. 20011	A listing of museums—and their publications—by states and cities. Look under headings: Art Galleries and Natural History Museums for bulletins, catalogs, journals.
READER'S GUIDE TO PERIODICAL LITERATURE R. R. Bowker Company 1180 Avenue of the Americas New York, NY 10036	A listing of popular magazines in the United States, with general articles.
ULRICH'S INTERNATIONAL PERIODICALS DIRECTORY R. R. Bowker Company 1180 Avenue of the Americas New York, NY 10036	Lists magazines by countries, with classifications by subject and by language; indicates if illustrated. Look under headings: Art, Anthropology, Archeology, Glass, Hobbies, Jewelry, General Interest and individual country sections.

Index